LOST
DAUGHTER

NOLA WUNDERLE

PHOENIX RISING PRESS

Copyright © 2013 by Nola Wunderle

National Library of Australia Cataloguing-in-Publication entry
Author: Wunderle, Nola.
Title.   Lost daughter : a daughter's suffering : a mother's unconditional love : an
          extraordinary story of hope and survival / Nola Wunderle.
ISBN: 9780992273408 (paperback)
Subjects: Wunderle, Kartya.
          Adoptees--Australia--Identification.
          Adoptees--Australia--Biography.
          Adoptees--Australia--Family relationships.
          Birthparents--Taiwan--Identification.
          Drug addicts--Australia--Biography.
          Drug addicts--Australia--Family relationships.
Dewey Number: 362.8298092

Publishing Details
Published in Australia – Phoenix Rising Press
nwunderle@bigpond.com

Printed & Channel Distribution in US/UK/Canada/Aus
Printed through Lightning Source (USA/UK/AUS)
Available via:
United States - Ingram Book Company; Amazon.com; Baker & Taylor and others
Canada - Chapters Indigo; Amazon Canada and others
United Kingdom - Amazon.com; Bertrams; Book Depository Ltd; Gardners; and others
Australia - Rainbow Book Agencies, The Nile; James Bennet, ALS, Dennis Jones
and Associates; Peter Pal, University Co-operative Bookshop, Booktopia.

Ordering Information:
Quantity sales. Special discounts are available on quantity purchases by corporations, associations, and others. For details, contact the "Publisher" at the email address above.

To my mother, Enid Irwin, who taught me, by example, everything about unconditional love.

To Li Meng, a birth mother to be proud of. Our lives have been enriched through finding you.

He who learns must suffer.
And even in our sleep - pain that cannot forget;
Falls drop by drop upon the heart,
And in our own despair
against our will,
Comes wisdom to us by the awful grace of God"

Aeschylus (525-456 BC)

Acknowledgements

I would like to acknowledge Bian Siu-leng, my birth father. I know that people may think that he did the wrong thing but seeing through my eyes and feeling through my heart, he did a wonderful thing in giving me a beautiful adventurous life. Meeting him would have been wonderful because then I could have learnt from both parents not one. I would have liked to have heard, from him, more about his life. From my birth mother and sister I will hear the stories of his life and then I feel that my journey of discovery will be complete. These stories will become memories that I will cherish forever. He will be in my heart and thoughts always.

Thank you to Fang Li-meng, my birth mother; Hsu Long-tong, my step father; Bian Jar-chi, my blood sister. It took a great deal of courage for my mother to come forward to meet me. The two weeks of knowing that I was her daughter would have been wonderful yet painful and sad at the same time. I will be forever grateful to her. Through meeting her I learnt that no matter what happens, good or bad, never give up what you are trying to achieve. My birth mother and sister taught me to keep going and I *will* keep going. As soon as I saw them in the early morning hours I knew instantly that they were the family that I had been searching for, for so long. I will love them forever and value every living moment we have together.

Without the public and media coverage I had in Taiwan, my reunion with my family would never have happened. I would not have the new life that I have today without their generosity. Taiwan opened up their hearts to me, prayed for me and helped make my dream come true. The Taiwanese public and media gave me the strength to continue searching for my mother, the one woman in a population of twenty-two million.

Last is the best. To the family that has the biggest heart in the world. The people who adopted me. My adopted mother has the courage and strength that will never die in her. I am positive she will live to 150. Why? Because of the amazing willpower and determination she has. Without her I wouldn't and couldn't have done it. My dreams would never have come true without her in my life.

To my adopted father, you are the man of my life. The man that I love the most, the man that I admire the most and the man that I will forever look up to and remember for eternity. Daddy, I am still your 'pumpkin' and I will always be your 'pumpkin'. I love you.

To Kiersten, my sister, you have always been there and you have always been the one that worries silently about your younger sister. Our sisterly bond can never be broken, you are my best friend. I love you, sis.

And to my brothers, Alex and Josh. Alex, you are also my best friend. You were always the one that knew what I was going through and you help put a smile on my face when I feel down. Love you, big brother. To my other brother, Joshua, we have both been through a lot together, thanks for understanding me, I love you too. And to one other person who has been in my life for many long years. It feels like forever. Misty, my best friend. You are the one I will never forget. We always help each other whenever we are in a crisis. We practically live our lives the same and we have been through so much together. You are a sister to me. I love you.

To everyone I have known and have been there for me, thank you for all the encouragement and advice you have given me. The advice and encouragement finally did pay off.

Thank you.

Kartya Elizabeth Wunderle

Firstly I would like to thank the very professional team at MBS Press who gave me so much encouragement and support. Especially Julie-Ann Harper, without your help, it would have made my job so much more difficult. You gave me the confidence to believe that I could do it. I will be eternally grateful. To the team at Expert Subjects, I thank you for your help and support. Nothing was too much trouble for you. William and Marija, I thank you.

To the many people who gave help and support to our family: Lisa Jacques from Harrison Youth Services; Grace Tink from Ringwood Extended Family Services; Chris Bull from Wesley Youth Services; Julie, Caroline and Jackie from Mitcham House; all the staff at Human Services, Juvenile Justice and Child Protection Departments, especially Ros Harris, Margaret Cook, Diane Hamilton and Jane Campbell

To Romduol, Heng, Sophea and Vichea for allowing me to

include their story. To my employer, Early Settler, in particular, my manager, Christine Newlove for your understanding and friendship. Thanks for giving me three months off work to write this book.

I will always be thankful for the love, support and advice of our adoptive mothers' dinner party group. You have all been a tower of strength to me over the years.

To Ian and Kathy Hyslop, for all your help in finding Kartya's mum. We could not have done it without you. You never gave up, for that we are grateful.

To George Gao and the staff at *United Daily News* in Taipei. Your enthusiasm was infectious. How could we ever forget your love and support?

To Julie Chu and husband, Tony. Thank you for meeting us and helping us to fulfill Kartya's dream.

To Cathay Pacific Airlines in Taipei for sponsoring our flight to Taiwan.

To Christian Piroden, General Manager of the Imperial Inter. Continental Hotel in Taipei. Thank you for your sponsorship and friendship.

To Yang Tzu-Ching, Commissioner of Interpol, Taipei and to Ke Ching-Chung, Senior Investigator, International Criminal Affairs Division, and to the Forensic Science Division. Your hard work was rewarded. What a magnificent job you all did.

To Sam Gerovich, Australian Commerce and Industry Office in Taipei. Thank you for your understanding and assistance.

For the mammoth task of organising the press conference, we must thank Pauline Leung, Chief Executive Officer of Compass Public Relations. Pauline, your generosity and sensitivity to Kartya's plight touched us all, you could not have done more to help us.

To Stephen Taylor, Liz Hayes and the crew of *60 Minutes*. Thanks for doing such a wonderful and moving story.

To my wonderful father, Lyle Irwin. Thank you for your love and support to our family and for never giving up on Kartya.

To all my brothers and sisters. I am proud to be part of such an interesting family. I love you all.

To Alexander and Joshua. You give me so much love, support and encouragement. Both of you are always there for me. I love you both more than words can express. You are legends.

To my very beautiful Kiersten. You were 'the wind beneath my wings' when I felt like giving up. You took care of me and loved me. I feel so blessed to have you and I love you very much. You are a star.

To my brave Kartya. You fought like a tiger for your right to find out who you are. Your journey of discovery has given you the inner peace you sought for so long. Thank you for your permission and trust in me to tell our story to inspire and help others. May your journey of recovery continue. We all love you unconditionally. You are a hero.

To the tall dark handsome man I have spent the last thirty years with. My husband, Othmar. I could not have survived without you. There is nothing I would change. Thank you for being my best friend and for being a father to be proud of. We all love you very much.

Nola Wunderle

Contents

Who Am I?

I really want to meet them
Being in suspense
It hurts me so much
That they didn't want me to know
WHO they are WHO are they?
What do they look like?
Being adopted is easy, but hard
Hard when you start to wonder!
I wish I could meet them
I cry at night
Wondering if they ever think about me
I want to find them
I need to find them
but no-one's helping me
WHO ARE THEY?
WHO are my parents?
When will you come and find me?
When will you wonder WHO I am?
One day my wish will come true
It's like being in a cage, being trapped
Like a prisoner inside of myself

Not knowing WHO I really am
or not knowing where I came from
Where are you? Will you ever come and find me?

Kartya

CHAPTER ONE

Meeting Kartya

We were all full of expectation as we waited impatiently at Melbourne's international airport. I hadn't slept properly for weeks. All of us had been waiting for this moment for months. Our fourth child was soon to arrive. Kiersten, particularly, was eagerly awaiting her little sister. She loved her two brothers, but a sister adopted just like she was would be very special.

What a mixed bunch we were. Me, the Aussie girl from Geelong. Othmar, the dad, born and bred in Germany. Kiersten from Vietnam, a Eurasian war orphan. Alex and Josh, half German and half Australian. Kiersten was six. Alex was five and Joshua two. And our newest addition was about to come through the airport gates: Kartya Elizabeth from Taiwan.

It had been almost five months since we had first set eyes on the photo of the little baby girl and fallen in love with her. It was the little fat face with the cupid's bow lips that I fell for. I felt like I had met her before and that she belonged with us. Our friends, Pat and Oscar, had brought the photo back from Taiwan. It had been given to them by Julie Chu, the lawyer organising the adoption. They had adopted a little girl, Sharn, two months before.

As we waited at the arrival terminal, I felt chilly. I don't know if it was due to the fact that it was an early autumn day in Melbourne or if it was the excitement of the event but the hairs on my arms stood up. I draped the pink baby blanket over my shoulders to warm my body. I kept glancing at the photo, as if to remind myself what she would look like. How could I possibly forget? I'd been carrying the photo in my purse for months. What a robust, healthy baby she appeared to be. Even at only four months she had a look of contentment and serenity about her. She would be nine months old now. My mind told me she would be a big fat healthy baby, almost ready to take us by the hand and walk us off to her new home. She would have been well cared for, I had no doubt about that, because we had paid extra money to the orphanage for top-quality nursery care. We wanted the very best for our baby.

I had butterflies in my stomach. My feelings were a mixture of excitement and fear. I hoped that she would like us. I hoped she would bond with us. And then I told myself that was a stupid thing to think. She was just a baby; of course she would love us. Othmar was squeezing my hand tightly assuring me that everything would be fine. I knew he was eager to hold his second daughter.

It seemed like everyone else in the world was bursting through the doors—but not the one we wanted.

'Mum, I wish they would hurry up,' said Alex. He'd been talking about this special event for weeks. He told his classmates in 'show and tell' that he was getting a baby sister off an aeroplane. He even took the little photo of Kartya to school to show his friends. I overheard one of them say, 'She doesn't look anything like a sister.'

Alex said, 'Of course she doesn't, silly, because she's adopted. But she's still going to be my sister.'

Michael and Susan, a couple we had met through an adoptive parents group, were bringing Kartya home to us. We had every confidence that they would take care of our baby during the flight. We had only met them twice but, like all the adoptive parents we knew, they were a warm, loving couple. They would be bringing their newly adopted daughter home, too. They had been in Taiwan adopting a little girl themselves. Through Community Services we obtained approval to do a proxy adoption. This meant we did not need to travel to Taiwan ourselves. It took longer than usual, though, because of all the official paperwork, nearly four months. However, our constant phone calls to and from Taiwan with Julie Chu, the lawyer, assured us that Kartya was well cared for.

Kiersten, Alex and Josh had each brought a soft fluffy animal for their little sister. My sister Nerida was there, poised with her camera, ready to record the special event. I couldn't help but think that it was more stressful than giving birth. Giving birth was easy for me. I loved being pregnant and the boys just popped out. No dramas. No waiting around, heart thumping, hand sweating in anticipation.

Oh, God, I suddenly saw Michael and Susan in the distance coming through the doors. Susan had a tiny bundle in her arms; it couldn't be Kartya, it must be her baby. The bundle was too small to be Kartya. My eyes scanned the crowd for Michael; he must have our baby. Our baby would be sitting up, looking around. I said to Othmar anxiously, 'That's not her, is it?' He shrugged his shoulders. Susan fought her way through the crowd of people, walked right up to me and handed me the tiny bundle. 'Congratulations, Mum. Here is your daughter.'

My mind was telling me that they had sent the wrong baby from Taiwan. She looked nothing like her photograph. What had happened to our baby? This couldn't be her. This baby only looked about three months old. Where was our big fat healthy baby? I held her in my arms and spoke out loud as the realisation began to dawn. 'Oh my God, you poor little thing, who did this to you? You are so small, what happened to you? Someone was supposed to look after you.' I scanned her face for any resemblance to the photo. I pulled the photo from my pocket and looked at it again. Yes, it was her, the tiny brown spot beside her eye was there, just like in the photo.

Alex rubbed his cheek on hers and asked, 'Mum, what's wrong with her? She looks sick.' Kiersten and Josh together hugged and squeezed her tightly. 'Mum, we'll make her all better, won't we?' said Kiersten. Othmar had his arms around us all. I looked at him and said, 'What do you think?' He just shook his head. Finally he said sadly, 'She does not look very well at all.'

Suddenly Kartya began to scream. She screamed and screamed as if she were in pain. She was rigid, stiff as a board. It felt like she was frozen in one piece. We were all still standing in the one spot; none of us had moved. Other passengers must have been made curious by this little group that was engrossed in this tiny screaming bundle. Several people stood and watched us. I was crying. I felt sad and happy at the same time. Othmar took Kartya in his arms and I just stood there, shaking my head, a condition that was to become quite common over the coming years. Whenever I became stressed, I would unknowingly start shaking my head, as if in disbelief. The kids named it 'Mum's shaking head syndrome'.

We all walked out of the airport to our car. I clutched Kartya close to my chest; her face was snuggled into my neck. She kept screaming. Othmar was holding Kiersten and Alex's hands. Joshua was holding the end of my skirt. Everyone's excitement was visible, with the kids chatting amongst themselves about who was going to have first turn to hold her. The sun was shining; it was going to be a beautiful day. I sat in the back seat with this little screaming bundle in my arms, trying to imagine the journey that we were all to travel with Kartya Elizabeth Wunderle. Despite my shock, as we drove back home through Melbourne's busy streets, my optimism and enthusiasm returned: we would make our baby well. I made a promise to her in my mind that nothing bad would ever happen to her again. Kiersten piped up in her little squeaky voice, 'Mum, maybe she'll stop crying if I give her my doll.' I thanked her for being thoughtful, but I felt that the sight of a black Cabbage Patch doll wasn't exactly what Kartya needed. I told myself that our family would love and protect her always.

I was overcome by love and pity for this little red-faced screamer and I felt that inside this tiny girl there was a story. A story that perhaps we would never know. I wasn't even sure that I wanted to know. I just wanted her to look like her photo again.

At home, we gingerly unwrapped our tiny bundle. She was skinny, scrawny and still screaming uncontrollably. Her little bottom was red raw, with huge weeping sores right up to her waist. I said to Othmar, 'Not much wonder she's screaming. How could this happen?' Michael and Susan didn't mention anything to us about her red raw bottom. Then again, we were so consumed with our new arrival, that we didn't really talk to them. We just said goodbye and promised to catch up.

We thought that Kartya might have been dehydrated from the flight, so we tried to give her a bottle, but she would not feed, she could not feed. She just screamed and lay rigid, like an ironing board. The beauty spot beside her eye was very evident. One ear looked as if it had been turned inside out.

My friend Barbara arrived with some flowers to welcome home our new baby. Barbara was a committee member of an adoptive parents group that Othmar and I had helped to form three years before. Barbara had a strong commitment to helping adoptive families and also a strong desire to adopt a child from overseas herself. She was such a warm, caring person that we all considered her a family member. We had a huge network of families with adopted children. Children from Vietnam, Thailand, the Philippines, Sri Lanka and now Taiwan. All of us parents looked upon all the adopted children as our own. We were always there to love and support each other.

Barbara took one look at Kartya and said, 'This kid should be in hospital, she's not well.' I was suddenly scared there was something seriously wrong with her, so we wrapped our new baby back up, piled back in the car and took her to Box Hill Hospital.

One of the first doctors to see Kartya was a young Asian intern named Dr Lim. He asked us why we had adopted a baby that wasn't healthy. He said, 'When you adopt baby, you should make sure you get healthy baby. This baby no good, she have big problems.' He also seemed to think it was a bit strange that we had adopted a baby when we could have our own.

Finally he told us that Asians would not adopt a child if they could have their own. When he said that Kartya would have to stay in hospital under observation, we were all devastated. We had waited so long for her, and now we had to leave her alone again. The doctor told us she was dehydrated, malnourished, had suffered enormous physical neglect and the sores on her buttocks were from not having her nappy changed over a long period of time. He also commented on the fact that her head was severely moulded indicating that she had been lying on it continually over a prolonged period. Othmar and I had noticed that when we looked at her side on, she appeared to have only half a head, as if the back of her head was missing. She needed expert help and we could not deny that she was in the best of hands to heal her fragile body. The nurses took a shine to her and assured us that they would take good care of her. They could see that we were all upset. As we walked slowly away from the hospital, Kiersten was crying so much that she got the hiccups. She said, 'Mum, it's not fair, why did she have to be sick? I just wanted to take her home, that's all.'

There are two things that make me sick more than anything: one is aeroplanes, the other is hospitals. But I couldn't wait to get to the hospital the next day. Overnight, I'd forgotten what she looked like. I just wanted to see her little face again. We all went in to the ward: Othmar, Alex, Kiersten and Josh, with me walking about ten steps ahead of them. In through the big automatic doors, into the lift, up to the second floor. I was hit by a wave of nausea. I felt like I was going to vomit. Every time I went into a hospital I felt the same way. It was the smell of food and disinfectant and the thought of blood. I could never stand the sight of blood.

Once Alex had fallen off his bunk bed, splitting his forehead open. I had taken him to the same hospital to have stitches. I fainted and the doctor put me on the bed next to Alex while he had his head stitched up.

Kartya was lying in a big white iron cot with the sides pulled up. Bits of paint were chipped off the side. I picked her up and cuddled her, but she didn't respond at all. The kids took turns holding her while we snapped lots of photos. Alex wanted to take them to school for show and tell to prove that he did get a sister.

I would spend every day at the hospital, sitting in the chair beside Kartya's cot, trying to will her back to health. She was detached and unresponsive. She looked so terribly sad. I would pick her up and cuddle her and she would look at me with such a lack of interest, as if to say: Who exactly are you supposed to be? When the other kids were about the same age as Kartya I could engage them in all sorts of fun play. I would blow kisses on their neck and they would shriek with delight. I would play the game 'round and round the garden, like a teddy-bear, one step, two steps, tickle me under there'. Even at ten months they knew that it was a funny game. Kartya didn't like my funny games at all. She would scream at me. She didn't even like it when I held her quietly and gently. She wriggled to get free from my grasp. I would try to give her a bottle, but the nurses said the only way she would feed was with it propped up on the pillows beside her. The only way she would sleep was flat on her back with her arms and legs spread-eagled.

Othmar and I had noticed that she had strange discolouration on her wrists and ankles. We wondered what had caused that. When I would hug her and hold her, she wriggled free as if to say, don't do that, I don't like it. She could stand up straight, but not sit down. Her legs were unable to bend. We felt helpless to take away the pain we knew she was experiencing. I could see it in her eyes. She had a shallow, glazed look of indifference. I would hold her, I would talk to her, I would stroke her face, but she never responded. She remained unreachable. I thought that we just needed time together, time to bond. My enthusiasm would not be thwarted. Eventually, I believed, we would be mother and daughter.

From the beginning Kartya responded more readily to Othmar. He could engage brief eye contact with her. In general, she seemed more interested in him than me.

The other children could not understand why their sister could not be with them. Five-year-old Alex stood at her cot one day, tears streaming down his face, saying, 'Mummy, I prayed last night for

God to make her better. I don't want her to die, I just want her to get better.' My heart went out to him. He was a sensitive little boy who had already formed a bond with Kartya, just as he had with Kiersten, and he wanted her home.

One day I walked into the hospital and Dr Lim was pricking the bottom of Kartya's feet with a needle. I asked him what he was doing and he told me he was testing her responses. She didn't react at all. He said that sometimes when babies have been without love and care for a long while, they can block out physical and emotional pain. I thought it was strange that this little girl would cry when you cuddled her but when she had a needle poked into her foot, she showed no reaction. I wanted to ask Dr Lim if he thought that she would suffer any long-term problems. I didn't, because I thought it would be a stupid question. After all, she was a baby, she would forget whatever happened to her. Besides, Dr Lim would tell me if she needed any special care in the future. I was sure of that.

Even though I was sad every day I left the hospital, I could see that she was getting better and stronger and that soon she would be able to come home. Going to the hospital every day and night was exhausting me. I still had the other three kids to organise. Kiersten and Alex were at school. I would take Joshua with me to hospital. He was nearly two years old and was happy to go and see 'his baby' every day.

Dr Mason, who took charge of Kartya's treatment, was an imposing-looking man in his early forties with grey hair and a black moustache. He would give me an update every day. He felt that she was coming along extremely well and would suffer no long-term effects from her unfortunate beginnings. Each day she got stronger, more alert and even on the odd occasion smiled.

Two weeks after admitting Kartya to hospital, we got permission to take her home. I was relieved that I didn't have to drive away from the hospital for one more day leaving Kartya behind. It had been very stressful for all of us. Her medical report read:

Taiwanese orphan admitted 21.3.1981. Nine-month-old baby had been adopted and her mother felt unhappy about the fact that the child was not feeding. No past history known. On examination, Kartya was a Chinese babe with head circumference, weight and length all well below normal. Her head was quite moulded, having been lying on it for past nine months. Assessment showed her to be at least four months old, although this is hard to assess due to cultural differences. Skin discolouration on wrists and ankles indicate that babe has been restricted in movement over a period of time. We discovered that babe would only feed and sleep lying flat on back. Total absence of eye contact would indicate severe emotional deprivation. Kartya is scrawny, immobile and febrile. No obvious cause of Failure to Thrive other than emotional deprivation and physical stimulation denied. Should have no problems bonding to enthusiastic, loving family

I packed up Kartya's soft toys, her little singlets and her other belongings into my overnight bag. I wrapped her up in her pink bunny rug. I wanted to get her out of the hospital as quickly as possible. She needed to be home with us, her new family. As we farewelled the hospital staff and thanked them, I asked Dr Mason how he thought Kartya got the marks on her wrists and ankles.

He said he believed that she had been tied to a cot to stop her from moving. That would explain why she would only sleep and feed on her back: that was all she was used to. I felt sick. How could anyone do such a thing to a defenceless baby?

The cure seemed pretty simple at the time: love would overcome everything. As we drove away from the hospital we were confident that the love that we all felt for her would surmount any difficulties we would encounter along the way.

The physical scars from Kartya's early mistreatment soon began to heal. The discolouration on her wrists and ankles started to fade. The horrible sores on her buttocks began to heal over. We did wonder occasionally if any of this pain and suffering could have left any emotional scars, but Othmar and I reassured ourselves that as she was so young she had every chance of healing completely.

I had always thought that bonding, for a small baby, was automatic. I had no problems with Alex and Josh, and with Kiersten it was instant. She was stuck like glue to me. The moment we set eyes on each other, we bonded. Our destiny was to be mother and daughter forever. With Kartya it was to be a very different story.

CHAPTER TWO

Babyhood

When Kiersten and Alex were babies, I had a practice of laying them on my tummy, face down. I would then wrap my big towelling dressing-gown around us and go to sleep flat on my back. They would instantly settle. It was so easy. I think it was the closeness and the heartbeat that soothed them. I practised the same procedure with Joshua when he was a baby. It was my magic formula for instant sleep. It worked every time.

For Kartya, nothing worked. She was stressed and miserable and unable to sleep. I would try the dressing-gown trick with her, but she would go crazy. She would kick and scream, she absolutely hated it. She could not stand to be physically close to anyone. It was as if her very life was at stake. The message she constantly gave us was: Don't hug me, don't you dare hold me tight, don't kiss me, I don't like it. At the time, both Othmar and I thought it was a bit unusual, but we felt that in time she would trust us enough to feel comfortable with the love we had to give her. The other three kids were very affectionate, so we had no doubt that Kartya would also accept our love and affection.

Physically, she thrived. Her body loosened up. She could bend her legs and sit normally. When I held her, I felt I was holding a baby and not an ironing board. Within three months, she was the chubby little girl we had expected to pick up from the airport. She loved food. She would eat absolutely anything. She would sit like a little bird with her mouth open all the time, waiting for someone to pop food into it. The more she ate, the more I fed her. Kiersten and Alex would take turns to feed her. She would sit up in her highchair and with each spoonful she would almost swallow the spoon.

From the very beginning Kartya bonded more successfully with Othmar. Her feelings for him, made obvious in hospital, continued to grow. Her eyes would light up when she saw him. He does have a special way with kids; they adored him. Kartya still kept her distance from me. It was as if she could take me or leave me. She would look at me with no interest at all, as if to say: Who is this person who is continually trying to be all lovey-dovey? Kiersten, Alex and Joshua treated her in a special way, maybe because she had been so sick. I think they felt lucky to have her. They would always be trying to do things to make her laugh, and that wasn't easy. They would get dressed in fancy dress and dance around her highchair until she was laughing. Alex would wear a Batman cape and leap up and down. He took things to extremes one day when he jumped off the garage roof and broke his arm.

Kartya was strong-willed and determined, stubborn and difficult. If she wanted her own way, she usually got it by screaming the house down until we all succumbed. When she was about fourteen months old she got an infection and needed antibiotics. Othmar and I tried everything to get her to swallow the medicine, but she just wouldn't take it. We were both holding her down, trying to open the side of her mouth to get the eyedropper in, but she kept her teeth clenched and screamed and kicked. There was no way she was going to let anything in her mouth. We finished up with medicine all over us, but none in Kartya's mouth. Her face was bright red with anger. If she had been able to speak, I'm sure she would have said: Don't you dare do something to me that I don't want. We took her over the road to our family doctor for an injection because he couldn't get the medicine in her mouth either. He flippantly commented, 'This young lady will give you a hard time with a temper like that.' Little did we know how hard.

So that we could hear her at night Kartya was still sleeping in her cot in our bedroom. She was not a good sleeper. She still slept flat on her back. I would wrap her up in her rug, lie her on her tummy, and tuck her in snugly. No sooner had I done that than she would be kicking everything off, as if to get free, then turning over and lying on her back, flat out, with her arms spread above her head. She also developed a habit of climbing out of her cot, especially in the middle of the night. Once she climbed out and I didn't hear her. Suddenly I heard some noises in the kitchen and flew out of bed. She had opened the refrigerator door, grabbed the milk containers and poured them all over the floor. The kitchen was on a bit of a lean and all the milk ran into the cupboards. It was three o'clock in the morning. She was wide awake. At times, I would think, this one child is more work than the other three put together.

Kiersten always played the little mother with Kartya. She loved her and didn't seem to mind cleaning up the chaos left by her little sister. They were such opposites: Kiersten, the sweet, gentle, affectionate, considerate little girl; Kartya, the strong, aggressive, angry, assertive little girl.

Othmar and I often thought of Kartya's birth family. We couldn't help but wonder who she took after. Obviously someone in her family was a strong person, with a mind of their own. Her adoption papers stated that she was named Lin-Mei-Li, third daughter of Lin-Ah-Hua. No father was named on the papers. We presumed that her birth mother was poor and unable to care for her. We felt sure that whatever the reason was, Kartya was now in good hands and that we would love and care for her and stick by her always. I was still determined and confident that one day she would love me.

Othmar and I never got over the shock of learning that Kartya had been tied by her wrists and ankles to a cot. In a way, I think we both felt an unconscious guilt for being in some way responsible for part of her suffering prior to us even setting eyes on her. We had believed that she was receiving the best nursery care money could buy, but, while waiting to come to us, she had been wickedly, unforgivably mistreated. We didn't know to what extent, only our imaginations could do that for us, but somehow our unwitting, unknowing collusion created in me an overwhelming need to protect her, to shield her from pain. If her birth mother had done this to her, then she was better off with us.

Kiersten, Alex and Joshua responded to love and affection; Kartya did not, could not. Kartya would have her running shoes on if it looked like a hug was on the way. She didn't seem to be able to let herself trust anyone. Her motto appeared to be: If I can't do it myself then I won't let anyone else do it for me. She wanted to do everything for herself. 'Mum, I can feed myself. Mum, I can dress myself. Mum, I can wash myself. Mum, I don't need you because I can be Mum to myself.' Her strong personality was evident right from the beginning.

Othmar and I often talked until all hours of the night about her independent nature. We felt there was a reason for it, that one day she would need it. It would be of some benefit to her, and we wanted to be able to channel it in the right direction. We had always believed that a child was a product of its upbringing and environment. As the years unfolded, we ate those words, one by one. We had not taken into consideration the genetic factor. With an adopted child there is always the unknown ingredient. There are things that they have to deal with that your biological children don't need to confront.

Othmar and I always felt that if our daughters wanted to find their biological families in the future we would help them. Our attitude regarding adoption was that it helps a child in need; when we became adoptive parents we were determined we would love that child as our own. If, in the future, we could reunite that child with their birth family members, then that was also our responsibility as adoptive parents. We believed this very strongly. Othmar and I could look at our families and know who we looked like. We could look at a mother and a father and brothers and sisters. This pleasure should not be denied an adopted child, if that was their wish. This is something we talked about and accepted even before we first adopted Kiersten. We felt a bond with the birth families because without them we would not have had our two little girls.

CHAPTER THREE

Nola's Childhood

People used to ask us, 'Why adopt a child when you can have your very own?' Our answer was always the same 'to give a child a family'. Somehow, though, I always felt that the real answer was a bit deeper than that.

I grew up as the fourth child in a family of ten. It was a pretty rugged and disciplined upbringing. We were a very poor family and my mother was the peacemaker in the family, the enforcer of family morals. Mum would have a jar with these little cubes of Velvet soap in it and, if we swore, she would hold our head over the bathroom sink and wash our mouths out with soap. We would have soapsuds foaming out of our mouth and nose. It was a strong incentive to be good and not swear at each other. All of us kids had very clean mouths.

My father was always out working. He worked nightshift as a security watchman and slept most of the day. On his days off, he would tinker with his car. He was always doing a grease and oil change or rotating his car tyres—never new ones, always retreads. He once built an overhead jack to winch one car engine out to replace it with another. He always enlisted the help of my older brothers to help him. They would stand around the car with Dad giving them orders. We were all a bit scared of Dad. He had a razor strap hanging beside the fireplace and if we were really naughty, punishment would be a few whacks on the backside or the back of the legs with the strap, more as a deterrent than anything else. When Dad was at home he was quiet and aloof; he only got involved in major transgressions.

We had a big paddock at the back of our house and we used to play in the grass. I would make daisy chains with my sister Lorraine and the boys would climb the trees. When we walked down the back lane the boys would be high up in the trees and they would spit on our heads.

I created my own little world, squished in the middle of all those kids. When I was about eleven, I asked my mother if I was adopted. I thought that if I was adopted, that would make me special. She said that I definitely was not adopted and why would I ask such a stupid question. With so many brothers and sisters I didn't feel very special, so I created my own identity and pretended to be adopted. That way I could imagine that I was really wanted and that my mum and dad had picked me out of a whole bunch of kids. I continued this fantasy for quite some time. However, every time we would go for a drive, my parents would go past Glastonbury Orphanage in Geelong and they would tell us, 'If you're naughty, that's where you'll finish up. All bad children get put in an orphanage.' Finally, I decided that if that was true, then I didn't want to be adopted any more.

As I grew up, I couldn't understand why anyone would willingly have all those kids. My best friend, Shirley, was an only child. Her clothes were always new. For her birthday she got a new bike. I thought she was so lucky.

The seed must have been planted in my mind around this time: one day, I would adopt some children and make them feel special.

We lived in a rundown weatherboard house in Geelong. It was an average suburban street with houses of a similar architectural appearance as ours, mostly home to one or two children—we were an exception with ten kids. Our house had lino on the floor and not much furniture, except for beds everywhere and dark brown blinds on the windows. The toilet was down the backyard. There were two sheds, one with a couple of dogs that got fed the leftover dinner scraps and the other with some chooks. We ate the chooks. Dad would chop their heads off with an axe and we would all go hysterical watching the chooks run around the backyard minus their heads. When they stopped running, Mum would put them in a bucket of warm salted water in the washhouse and we would have to pluck off the feathers. The little feathers would get stuck to our hands and the smell was disgusting. We hated doing it because it would make our hands all red and stinging.

I shared a bedroom with two of my brothers and my eldest sister. My sister Lorraine and I slept in a single bed together. We used to take turns to draw pictures on each other's backs with our fingers and we had to guess what the other was drawing. Lorraine was a good sister, she always let me play the game first. By the time it was her turn, I'd be asleep and she'd miss out. If we got cold, we would just put a few extra coats on the bed. We never had enough of those boring grey blankets with red stitching on them. Everything around the house was colourless. Dirty, grey-coloured walls, dull cream curtains with brown blinds; everything was so dark and dingy. I would make pictures in my mind of bright colourful images. I'd pretend that the walls had beautiful big pink roses and ribbons entwined around them. I pretended the lino on the floor had a leopardskin print. The curtains were all shiny, with pinks and greens and little purple violets all over. My favourite colour was pink. I could pretend that I was wearing all these wonderful colours, but most of the time I was wearing someone else's hand-me-downs in a dull grey or brown. I hated those colours. I imagined that one day I would be a famous fashion designer or an interior decorator. I would decorate rich people's homes in all the colours I liked.

I think I got my love of bright colours from my mum. She always liked nice things, even though she never had any money to buy very much. She had one dress that had all these bright red poppies all over it, and she would put in on just before dad got home, when he was on dayshift. She would go into the bathroom and comb her thick, black curly hair and put on her bright red lipstick. When I think of my mum, I picture her sitting at the kitchen table, looking beautiful with her bright red lips, a bottle of beer on the table, ready for my dad who any minute would walk up the steps through the front door. I always thought she was beautiful, with her big brown eyes that lit up and crinkled at the side when she smiled. I would love it when people told me that I looked like her. I wanted to be like her, and tuck my kids into bed at night, like she did. Every night she would say, 'Kids, into bed now and I will come and tuck you in.' She would kiss us on the forehead. She had a very gentle, caring side to her nature. We always knew that she loved us. It wasn't until years later that the thought occurred to me that it wasn't just me she tucked in and kissed on the forehead every night, but all ten of us.

My favourite things were an Enid Blyton book that I read over and over—it was the only book I had—and my pink satin ribbon.

I loved that ribbon. I would tie it in a big bow on top of my head. I would wash it and iron it and sleep with it under my pillow. It was the nicest thing I had.

My dad had this old car called a Mayflower. It was bright red. It looked like a station wagon with perspex windows and it was open at the back. On Sundays we always went for a drive. Mum and dad and my baby brother, Philip, would be in the front, and all of us kids would be packed in the back, sitting on bench seats dad had pulled out of some car wreck. Dad would drive around the Great Ocean Road at a huge speed. In the back, we were all terrified because the drop down to the ocean was about a hundred metres and we would imagine that he was going to miss a turn and go over the edge and we'd all hurtle down the hill into the ocean below. My brothers would be teasing us girls, saying, 'We're going to crash, we're going to crash.' Then they would start throwing up, all over them and us. My dad would stop for a short break, we would all pile out of the car, Mum would clean the boys up, and then out would come the Vegemite sandwiches and the raspberry cordial. Dad would drink his two bottles of beer, then we would be off once more, back home around the Great Ocean Road. My brothers throwing up again, red cordial all over our Sunday best clothes of white T-shirts, white shorts and white runners. You'd think we were all decked out to run a marathon. They were the only good clothes we had, but we always felt so clean and fresh and were very proud of ourselves. Mum was proud of us, too. She would pull out her treasured box brownie camera and take a photo of us all lined up in order of height. Tallest down to smallest.

Every Sunday night we would have a bath. Our big clean-up for the week. One bath cleaned everyone. Mum would boil the water in a big copper in the wash-house and carry it by the bucket load to the bathroom. She would fill the bath and then just top it up after each kid got out. I hated it because the boys always got in the bath first; us girls were always last. When we had all finished, the boys took great delight in telling us 'Guess what, girls? We pissed in the bath.' They would be falling all over the place laughing, and us girls would be crying, begging Mum for another bath. We would all be bundled into bed with our weekly pair of clean pyjamas on and a nice, clean, stiff unbleached calico sheet on top of us. The used top sheet was now transferred to the bottom, covering the lumpy kapok mattress. My brothers would amuse themselves in bed by having a competition on who could fart the loudest. I always vowed that I would never marry a boy like my brothers.

When I was about twelve, my eldest brother Ken left home. I got his bed. I didn't have to share with my sister any more. A bed of my very own, a pillow of my own, and I could have his share of the overcoats to keep me warm.

My brother went off and joined the Navy. My mum cried for weeks. I couldn't understand why—I thought she'd be happy with one less mouth to feed. When he would come home on leave she would spoil him. She would cook him anything he wanted. We all envied him, because he would sail to Hong Kong and other exotic places. He would get shirts specially made for him. He would always bring home presents for Mum. One of her favourites was a big black photo album with mother-of-pearl inlay on the front cover. Mum thought she was very special and rich with such a beautiful album. She would spend hours putting black and white photos of us kids in it. She would stick them down with little black corners. We thought our brother Ken was rich, being in the Navy. Mum would press his special bellbottom trousers with a big wet cloth. They had all these special creases in them. When he put them on, she would check to see that they sat right and that the creases were all in the right spot. Mum was so proud of him, her son in the Navy travelling the world on a big ship.

The day after my fifteenth birthday, my mum said to me, 'Nola, tomorrow you can leave school.' I didn't want to, but I had no choice. Mum said, 'You must go to work; we need the money.' She got the newspapers and applied for three different jobs for me. One of them was an assistant's position in an interior decorator's shop and, after an interview, I got the job. I loved it because I could look all day at the bright fabrics that I had dreamed of, and feel their fineness between my fingers. I was allowed to take the remnants home. At night I would handsew clothes for myself out of shiny materials covered with violets and roses. We didn't have a sewing machine, we were too poor, but my mum had a big glass jar filled with all these buttons. Big, small, pearl, glass and every colour of the rainbow. I think she saved them. Maybe it was her hobby. If we were really good, we were allowed to play with them. My sisters and I would divide them into groups of colour and size. Every Thursday I would get my pay envelope. I would take it home unopened, and give it to mum and she would give me enough money for my bus fare for the next week and a little for myself. I never knew how much money I got paid. I didn't question it. I had to hand it over; I had no choice.

Mum didn't like any of us girls to wear make-up, she thought it looked cheap. I loved it. When I got to work each morning, I would put on my Candy Pink Starlet lipstick with black pencil around my eyes, and I would take it off on the bus on my way home. One day, I forgot to wipe it off. I walked in the front door at home. Mum took one look at me and gave me an almighty slap across the face. She called me a brazen little hussy, pulled me by the ear into the bathroom and washed my face. I was furious. I said to my mother, 'If I have to give you all my money each week, then the least I can do is wear make-up.' She didn't say anything. The next morning, I defiantly put on my Candy Pink lipstick and the black eyeliner that I had bought with the 'little for myself ' money, and went to work. We never spoke about it again.

I always wanted to leave home. Mum and Dad said that we had to stay home and pay board until we were twenty-one. I would count down the years, one by one. By the time I was nineteen, my eldest sister and two of my brothers had got married and left home. It was my turn to get the bungalow in the backyard. I was so excited. It was a little one-room shed, with fibro walls, louvre windows and sea-grass matting on the floor. I moved my few treasured possessions into that little room. It had a single bed and a wardrobe with my very own mirror. I made a cover for my bed out of a shiny piece of material with little ribbons and pink roses over it. That room became my refuge. For the first time in my life I had my own room. The only drawback was that in the winter the room got so damp and cold that condensation formed on the ceiling and drops of moisture would fall on me in the night. My clothes would go mouldy and my bed would feel damp. Also, the room was infested with earwigs, little long black bugs with tentacles. I would pick them out of my bed every night, and wake up in the morning with them crawling over my head and pillow. I would stuff cotton wool in my ears so that they couldn't crawl in. Still, I figured it was a small price to pay for some privacy. Every morning, my mum would knock on my door, or sometimes I would hear her take a jump from the back steps on to the bungalow steps to wake me. She'd be standing there with a cup of tea and Vegemite on toast cut in fingers. It was her way of showing that she cared.

Every night when I got home from work, my mum had my dinner ready. It would be sitting on the sink with a saucepan lid on top. Then she'd put it in the oven to heat it up. She was a good mum, always looking after her children. That's all she ever did. She didn't have any outside interests. Looking after her ten kids was her life. There was no time or energy left for anything or anybody else. I would look at my mum and think to myself, I never want to be like this, just looking after kids all my life, being poor, not being able to do anything else with my life.

My sister Lorraine gave me a party for my twenty-first birthday. Mum and Dad gave me a marcasite watch. It was really beautiful. They had saved for months to buy it for me. The day I had been counting down to had finally arrived. The next day I left home. My mum and my sister Lorraine drove me to Melbourne, to a mansion in Toorak where I had a job as a nanny. They said goodbye to me and sat out the front in my sister's car for an hour or so, crying. They didn't really want me to leave. Again I thought my mum would be happy with one less mouth to feed.

I had to leave home. All my friends were getting pregnant and living in housing commission houses. I didn't want to end up like them. Worst of all, I didn't want to end up like my mother; poor, with ten kids.

Chapter Four

Othmar, Marriage and Children

$\mathcal{G}$ thought all my Christmases had come at once when I met Othmar. I had been to a restaurant for dinner, with a new-found boyfriend. A very charming waiter had served us. He was tall, dark, handsome and spoke with an accent. I couldn't take my eyes off him. Every time he came to our table, I smiled at him with my eyes. He got the message because he looked at me with some degree of interest. Towards the end of the evening, I made a trip to the ladies' room and wrote my phone number on a piece of paper with a message: 'If you like me as much as I think you do, ring me tomorrow.' As I walked past the good-looking waiter, I put the note on his silver tray. On the way out, I turned and smiled at him. I didn't even know his name. With that, I left with my friend.

The next day was a Sunday. I was in bed asleep, when my

flatmate called out to me, 'Nola, phone. It's some guy with an accent.' I flew out of bed and picked up the phone. It was him. He said, 'Good morning, this is Othmar here.'

He invited me to dinner that night at a very swish upmarket restaurant called 'Eliza's'. I spent all day getting ready. I tried on about ten different outfits trying to look perfect for my big date. Othmar came to pick me up in a taxi. I opened the door and there he was in his cream suede jacket, matching trousers and a shiny cravat around his neck. His black curly hair was all swished back. God, I thought he was handsome. I was all dressed up in my little high-neck, powder blue, Laura Ashley dress, my white fur lapin jacket around my shoulders, my favourite Candy Pink lipstick on and my hair piled high on top of my head in curls. Othmar took one look at me, and said, 'Oh, I'm sorry, didn't I tell you it was casual dress?' I felt really stupid, but I pretended that the comment didn't upset me. Obviously he thought I was a tad overdressed. Maybe it was the white lapin coat.

We were given a lovely candle-lit table right on the dancefloor. The table was set with all these knives and forks. I had no idea which one you were supposed to use first. In Geelong with Mum and Dad we only ever had one knife and one fork, not a whole cutlery set beside your plate. I decided to wait and see which ones he used first. A waiter came to our table, all dressed up in a long white apron and bow tie, and handed us some menus. We looked at them for a while. Othmar said, 'What do you like? Any favourites?' I answered, 'I like the look of them all.' The fact that I didn't recognise any of them was a bit of a worry. Perhaps he sensed my discomfort so, being the gentleman that he was, Othmar said, 'Would you like me to order for both of us?' I thought, thank God for that. He ordered in a foreign language that I later learnt was German. I didn't know what he had ordered. I was starving. I hadn't eaten all day due to the excitement. Finally along came the waiter with a tray for each of us with little things in shells. I had no idea what they were. I pretended to recognise them as if they were my favourite dish and eventually Othmar said, 'Oh, I hope you like oysters kilpatrick.' I looked at them and said, 'Love them. Absolutely love them.'

I sat there, wondering what I was supposed to do with them. Was I meant to chew them up or just swallow them? At first I tried chewing them, but they kept slipping around my mouth. Then I tried to swallow one, but I imagined it was someone's eye, and it just came up again. I decided to just keep them in my mouth. Othmar was doing all the talking, so all I did was smile with my mouth closed and nod my head. When I had six of the little devils in my mouth, I was almost dry-retching. Without opening my mouth I gestured I needed to go to the ladies' room. I went to the toilet and spat them all out. I couldn't understand how anyone could seriously like oysters. You can't chew them and you can't swallow them. I went back to our table and proceeded to poke the remaining offenders into my mouth. Othmar was talking away about all sorts of things. I couldn't participate because my mouth was full of oysters. I think he thought I was mute. Occasionally I would nod my head. Then off I went to the toilet again and disposed of the last of the foreign bodies from my mouth. As I walked back to the table, I thought, at least I know what the little fork is for.

I found Othmar fascinating. He was so interesting. He talked about the stars and the planets, Pluto and Mars, and all sorts of things and places I never knew existed. He had this wonderful accent and lovely smooth hands, as if they had been manicured. He was nothing like my six brothers. I made up my mind that night that I would marry him.

The waiter came to our table with our main course. Thank God, I thought, some real food. It looked like a nice little steak on the plate. I waited for Othmar to start, so I would know which knife and fork to use. Suddenly I realised: you work your way from the outside in. I had just started to cut into my nice little steak with a serrated knife when, to my horror, these little things slid out. Othmar said, 'I hope you like carpetbag steak?' I thought, God, not more oysters. I couldn't get up and go to the toilet again, he'd think I was a right nut. I tried to squash the oysters with my fork, but they just slid around the plate. In the end, I popped them in my mouth, and coughed them into my serviette and then put it in my gold Oroton bag.

We drank Mateus rosé all night. Othmar told me how it was made and where it came from. He was so clever. I ate all my steak, even though I didn't enjoy it. Medium rare, with blood running out of it, was not my choice. I couldn't stand the sight of blood. I thought it was still half alive. The vegetables were good—I thought that mum's lumpy mince stew was better. I missed my mum's cooking. She would have been proud of me, though, sitting in an upperclass restaurant, using all these knives and forks, with an educated gentleman.

I half-expected to get oysters for sweets. I scanned the pancake but, to my surprise, not an oyster in sight. I now knew what the last knife and fork were for. At home we ate sweets with a spoon. Later, we danced the night away to Frank Sinatra and Perry Como. Othmar was such a smooth dancer. We did the cha-cha. I was good at following his feet. He was acting all suave and European, swinging me around the floor, whispering in my ear, telling me I was beautiful. He spoke about places in the world that I'd never heard about. I pretended that I knew them all. I didn't want him to think that I was dumb. Not me, in my best dress with my hair piled high on my head in curls. The curls were falling out, one by one.

I took him home to Geelong to meet my mum and dad. They loved him from the very beginning. Eighteen months later, I asked him to marry me; after all we'd been living together for six months and he'd never mentioned marriage. One night when he came home from work, I said, 'Are you ever going to marry me?' He casually replied, 'Can you wait a couple of weeks, so we can organise it?' When I asked him why he had never mentioned it before, he said he was going to ask me one day, he'd just never got around to it. I said, 'If you marry me, can we adopt some kids?' Much to my surprise, his immediate answer was, 'Maybe. I'll think about it.' I had often talked about adoption and I knew that Othmar was thinking about it. I knew that he needed time to think about it, but I also knew that if he did agree, that it would be a lifelong commitment. I was glad he didn't say 'Yes' straight away. I knew he needed time to think about it.

One month later we got married and he whisked me away overseas to all the places he had told me about. We travelled on a big luxurious Italian cruise ship called the *Marconi*. It took twenty-eight days to reach Genoa in Italy. We spent our time lazing around the swimming pool, playing table tennis and quoits. Every morning when I awoke, I had to pinch myself to make sure that I wasn't dreaming. I thought I was such a lucky girl. My tall, dark, handsome husband looked after my every need. Most of the time I was scared, though, because I couldn't swim. I would dream that the ship would sink and I didn't have a life belt on.

Finally we arrived in Europe. First off, we went to Othmar's home town of Frankfurt in Germany. I met his mum and dad, his brother Joachim and sister Monica. I loved his mum and dad straight away; they welcomed me and treated me like a daughter.

I became another member of their family. They were very warm, deeply religious people. His mum fussed over me, making sure all the time that I was happy. Othmar was translating their every word, making sure that I didn't miss out on anything. It was quite exhausting for him.

Othmar and I travelled all over Europe. My favourite place was Belgium. His brother and sister-in-law lived in Brussels. To me it was the sort of European town that I had imagined, with its cobbled streets, little outdoor cafes, wonderful shops and people dressed in beautiful clothes. After six months we got on another Italian liner called the *Donnizetti*, and went to Peru. Othmar had always wanted to visit South America. He said he wanted to live there, but I wasn't that sure. I still missed my mum and dad.

We moved into a nice little flat in Lima and made ourselves at home. Othmar got a job in a restaurant mixing cocktails. I stayed at home and played the good housewife, just like my mother. I loved it, I was very happy. We made a lot of friends, mainly German nationals, working in Peru. It was a busy bustling city, with either very rich people or very poor. No middle class. I could never work out which category we were in. After about eight months, I'd had enough. One night, Othmar came home from work and I was crying. He said, 'What's wrong?' Through my sobs, I said, 'I want to go home'. He put his arms around me, and said, 'Yes, so do I'.

The next day we booked our passage on the next available ship to come back to Australia. It had been a trip of a lifetime. I had travelled the globe. I'd seen places and people I'd only ever dreamt of. The girl from Geelong had come up in the world. At least I wasn't living in a housing commission home with half a dozen kids.

It was while we were in Lima that I really got to know this tall, dark, handsome man with the foreign accent whom I had married, vowing to love him for richer or poorer, through sickness and health, till death do us part. I did add my own little vow at the end that went: And if it doesn't work out, we'll just get divorced. The thought of spending my whole life with the same person was a bit scary. I wanted an escape clause, just in case. Still, I was optimistic—as long as he would agree to adopt. If he could agree to this, then it would all work out just fine. He was still thinking about it, so that was a promising sign.

I had no doubt that he would make a good father; he had all the right qualities. He loved kids, he was caring about other people's thoughts and feelings. He came from a warm, close-knit family. He had very strong religious beliefs. He was very smart; he knew about everything. There was nothing that Othmar didn't know the whole story about. He would be able to teach our future children all about the seven wonders of the world, backwards, in two languages. He believed that all people were equal, no matter what race or religion they were. He had chosen to marry me and that made me believe that he was a very good judge of character. I asked him once, 'Othmar, what is it that you like about me?' With a smile on his face, he replied, 'You're not at all shy and you have a very loud voice.' I did have a voice, I wanted to be heard, even when no-one was listening. The legacy of growing up with nine brothers and sisters guaranteed you a loud voice, otherwise nobody heard you.

Othmar grew up in war-torn Germany. He was born on Hitler's fiftieth birthday. When his mother went to register his birth, an official suggested that it would be the proper and correct thing to add an 'Adolf' to her new son's name. She didn't want to, but she was pressured into it. They didn't really like Adolf all that much;

they disagreed with his teachings. When Othmar was about seven, he came home from school one day to find a man in a uniform sitting at the kitchen table. His mother said, 'Othmar, this is your father.' That's the first memory he had of his father, who had been at the Russian front, fighting in the Second World War.

They lived in a two-storey house in Offenbach and, as young children, they had been drilled by their mother and grandmother that when the sirens sounded, everyone got up, grabbed their gas masks and headed for the bunkers. The bomb shelters were huge above-ground community halls, holding up to one thousand people. They were equipped with bunks, toilets and an infirmary for the sick and elderly. The outside walls were about two metres thick with steel reinforcement and concrete, made to withstand the force and destruction of the bombs. Just before Christmas in 1943, they were ensconced in the bunker, listening to the bombs being dropped around them. Othmar's father poked his head out of the bunker just in time to see a bomb dropping on their house. It was his fortieth birthday. After this happened, the whole family was transported to a relative's farm in Reimlingen, a small town in southern Bavaria, from where the family originated.

As young children Othmar, his older brother Joachim and older sister Monica could see bombs being dropped by the Allies on a town not far from where they lived, called Nördlingen. In 1947, when their father was discharged from the services, the family moved to Frankfurt, to try and re-establish their lives. Othmar had problems relating to this man in a uniform who was his father. A father he didn't even know. The one person who gave him all the love and affection he needed was his grandmother; she spoilt her youngest grandchild. Oma always protected him. Life was not easy for them in Frankfurt after the war, as food products were not plentiful. They ate a lot of bread and pumpkin, but meat was very scarce. On Othmar's first communion feast, all his mother could get were two tins of goulash, even though she had asked the butcher three months in advance for meat.

When Othmar was nineteen, he left home. He joined the Navy, just like my brother. He was sent off to Sylt Island and from there they sent him to the Baltic Sea.

When he turned twenty-two he left the Navy and got a job at Frankfurt Airport. There he met a young man who had just come back from Melbourne. He told Othmar all about Australia. He said, 'All you need is ten pounds and you can go and live there for two years.' Othmar thought that would be a wonderful adventure, so he told his parents, 'I'm off to Australia.' They were not very impressed. To them, Australia was the end of the world, too far away to even be considered part of their world. They didn't want a son of theirs galavanting halfway around the world. They were afraid they would never see him again.

Nevertheless, he left. He arrived in Australia and lived with the parents of the young man he had met at the airport in Frankfurt. They were Greek, and they fed him lamb and cabbage, which he absolutely hated. He missed his European delicacies. He needed to learn a new language and a new culture. He desperately missed his mother's meals of *eisbein* and *sauerkraut*, *schnitzels* and fried potatoes, tongue and parsley sauce. His first job was with General Motors Holden on the assembly line. He decided after not too long that he didn't want to be doing that for the rest of his life so, when he was offered a job in hospitality, he grabbed it. With his new language skills he suddenly found himself working in one of Melbourne's best restaurants. It was there that he met the girl from Geelong who promised to take care of him, just as his mother had, and cook him *eisbein* and *schnitzels* and tongue. After much deliberation and very serious thought, he decided that he couldn't do better, so when she proposed to him one night, he accepted. He thought it was pure luck to find a girl who was prepared to take control over the important things in life. Just like his mother, who was always the one in control. Even though his father thought he was, everyone knew he wasn't.

I was a photographer. I would go around to people in the restaurants and ask them if they wanted a photograph taken, then I would go into my darkroom and develop and print them and take them back to the customer and sell them. It was a very good business. We both worked nights. Othmar worked in a restaurant, and I worked as a photographer. My young sister Nerida would come up from Geelong to help me. We would both go around to the tables in a German restaurant and take photos of people celebrating a special occasion. It was the 1970s and we had a very comfortable life. Othmar had come to the decision that he would like to adopt a child. We had talked about it many times; sometimes we'd be up till the early hours of the morning, discussing the commitment that we would both need to protect the best interests of the child we would adopt. With an abundance of enthusiasm, we applied to the Victorian Health and Community Services Intercountry Adoption Department to be assessed for an approval to adopt a child from overseas. We went through a lengthy assessment procedure, which included police checks, health checks, financial investigation and character references and we were told by our social worker that we were very good people. Apparently not good enough to adopt a child, though. We received a rejection letter in the mail. They said we should have our own baby first because we may not want to adopt after having our 'very own' child. We were angry. We didn't agree with that way of thinking. We decided that we would go ahead and adopt a child anyway, with or without approval. We had been told by a solicitor friend that we could go to another country and proceed to adopt a child legally in that country. He informed us of the legal papers that we would need to take with us, so we slowly started to gather all the information.

Adoption was my first priority. My thinking was that anyone can give birth: it takes a special parent to love someone else's birth child. I wanted to be a special parent and make my adopted child special. Othmar and I had often discussed how many children we would like to have. We decided that if we could adopt two and have two together, we would consider that perfect. When I got pregnant with Alex, we were on our way to fulfilling our dream of a family. I would dream about this little bundle in my tummy, and imagine this little dark-haired pretty boy, just like his father.

Even though I was pregnant, adoption remained very much on our minds. When we heard the news about Vietnamese war orphans, we both knew this was our chance. Once we decided that our adopted baby would come from Vietnam, everything happened quickly. Othmar got all the necessary paperwork to do an overseas adoption within a week and immediately he was off away overseas to a war-torn country to adopt our little boy or girl. I thought he was so brave to go over there, alone, with war raging. I worried about him.

Before Othmar left, we had discussed that maybe an older child would be best for us, perhaps a two-or three-year-old. After Othmar had been in Vietnam for about a week, I got a telegram from him, it read:

Kiersten . . . four months . . . beautiful . . . love Othmar.

I remember reading and thinking he'd made a mistake. He meant four years, I thought. She couldn't be four months. But she was. We were about to have two babies at once. We hadn't even had one, and now we were going to have two. Kiersten arrived in Australia one month later, flown out of Vietnam by the Australian Government airlift of orphans during the fall of Saigon. The prime minister at the time, Gough Whitlam, organised the flight on compassionate grounds, to help the orphans find new families. The babies like Kiersten who were registered with the Australian Embassy in Saigon were automatically flown to Australia. We went and picked her up from Berry Street Babies' Home in East Melbourne where she had been taken to by the Government.

The minute I laid my eyes on Kiersten, I loved her completely. I felt she was meant to be with us from that very moment. We bonded with her and she bonded with us immediately. She clung to me from the very beginning. If I left her for five minutes, she would be fretting. How she loved to be wrapped in my dressing-gown, lying on my chest, to go to sleep. When we first got her, we thought she might have been brain-damaged. She would just lie in her cot and look at the ceiling and roll her eyes and scream. I would pick her up, hold her close to my chest and she would stop. Some days I would tie her to my chest with a big sheet. She needed to be close to me all the time. It took about two months for her to stop screaming. I would get up in the middle of the night and sit beside her cot and watch her sleep. She was so beautiful and fragile. I would get a little mirror and put it in front of her mouth, to check if she was breathing. She couldn't stand any sort of noises. Especially the sound of a lawnmower. We thought it reminded her of the bombs dropping. For months she seemed confused about her environment. Then, one day, she smiled at me. I was so excited I rang Othmar at work and said, 'Guess what? Kiersten smiled at me.' We were both so happy.

Kiersten was a beautiful little girl. She was affectionate and loving. After her initial settling-in time, she thrived and became a very happy contented baby.

When Kiersten was five months old, I went into hospital to give birth to Alex. I wanted to take Kiersten with me, but the hospital wouldn't let me. Othmar looked after her. After twelve hours of labour I produced this nine-pound baby boy. He didn't look at all like the baby I thought was inside me. He was this big, fat, bald-headed, red-faced baby. I thought that the nurses had got the babies mixed up but, when I held him in my arms, it felt right. He felt like my baby. We took him home and introduced him to his big sister, Kiersten, except that newborn Alex was bigger. I would take them shopping in a twin stroller. An old lady came up to me one day and said, 'Oh, what beautiful twins.' I was tempted to tell her to go and get her eyes tested for new glasses. I agreed with her and smiled to myself. 'Twins'. Big, fat, bald Alex and little fragile Kiersten with black shoulder-length hair. No, they did not look like twins.

I didn't go back to work. I thought I would miss being a photographer and having my own business, but I didn't. I was happy being a mother. That's what I really wanted to do. To be a good mother, just like mine had been. When Kiersten and Alex were nearly two, I became pregnant. Othmar and I were both very happy. Our family was half complete. Joshua was born. A beautiful, contented baby came into our family. When Josh was twelve months old, we applied to adopt another child from overseas. To make sure that I would not get pregnant again, Othmar and I decided that it would be best for me to have a tubal ligation. I went along to my obstetrician and told him of our decision. He didn't want to do it. He thought that I was too young. He said that I would have to have a very good reason. I said, 'We do. We want to adopt another child.'

CHAPTER FIVE
Home Sweet Home

The home that Othmar and I created for our family was the opposite to the one that I had grown up in as a child. It was to become like the one I dreamt of when I was little. It was a big old rambling weatherboard house in a leafy green outer suburb of Melbourne. It had a quarter-acre garden. It was a haven for kids. There were big trees and lots of plants and flowers. The cottage garden had lavender, hollyhocks, daisies, petunias, begonias and lots of plants we couldn't even identify. The house was over a hundred years old and had all the charm and character of another era. I introduced all the colours and fabrics that I had pretended were in our house when I was a little girl at home with Mum and Dad. I had big red Persian-style rugs all over the polished boards in the lounge room. It was a huge room, like a ballroom. Othmar put up our big chandelier. It all looked very grand. We had a big antique sideboard and our dining table and chairs and a big old

Jacobean lounge suite. It was wall-to-wall furniture. It was warm and cosy and, most of all, colourful. In winter, Othmar would make a big fire in the open fireplace and the kids would sit around eating cut up bits of fruit and drinking hot chocolate.

Othmar's and my bedroom was like an inside garden. It was all roses. Roses on the bedspread, roses on the chests of drawers, roses on the curtains. Everything was covered in the same fabric, black background with big pink roses. When I got a bit stressed, I would go into the bedroom and lie on our bed and look at all the colour and I would feel more relaxed.

Alex's room was a big enclosed balcony with louvre windows all the way around. I made bright green curtains out of hospital sheeting to cover all the windows. Joshua had a red, white and blue room with bunk beds. There was always room for a friend to stay overnight. Kartya's room was my greatest achievement. It was perfect for a little girl, with creamy brown cottage wallpaper on the walls and a little brass and iron bed painted to match. There was a big fluffy Austrian curtain on the window that you could pull up to the ceiling. She could lie in bed and see the sky. There was a matching patchwork bedspread on her bed. It was in all shades of brown and cream with white trim everywhere. She did love her room. She would take food in there and hide it. Once I found a piece of chicken in her bedside drawers. I went to take it out and she screamed, 'Mummy, don't take it away. Please leave it.' I asked her why and she said, 'I might need it when I get hungry.' She was always hoarding food. I had to go into her room all the time to check for rotting bits of meat. Food was her comfort and security. She always had to have some in her hands, even though half the time she didn't eat it.

Kiersten had her own room. It had a small balcony overlooking the front garden. It featured an open fireplace and big windows that let in the light through the white lace curtains. She had an iron bed painted pale green, with a patchwork bedspread that matched her wallpaper of white with little pink and green flowers on it. It suited her, this quiet-natured little girl. She would do anything to please me. I would often think about her birth family; they must have been very peaceful, gentle people—she got her tranquil personality from someone. Everyone who knew Kiersten loved her. One day we were talking about her adoption and she said to me, 'Mummy, I'm glad that I didn't come out of your tummy.' I asked her why and she said, 'Because if I did, then you and Dad wouldn't have been able to adopt me'. That's the way she always thought, she adored me and Othmar. To Kiersten we were always Mum and Dad, she never wanted anyone else, just us.

Alex and Josh thought that it was normal to have adopted sisters. Most of our friends had biological and adopted kids. We would have family get-togethers once a month, where all the families would meet at a park and we would have a barbecue. These friendships developed from our involvement with our adoptive parents' group. No doubt we looked a mixed group of people with our kids from all over the world. On one occasion when Othmar and I were sitting around with our four kids, an elderly lady came up to us and asked us where our children came from. After explaining the background of each child, she commented, 'Why would you adopt, when you can have your own children?' I just looked at her and said, 'Why not?'

Our kids grew up knowing lots of other kids from different countries. We would take them to cultural events that were relevant to their country of birth to try and make them aware of their backgrounds. Most of the time the kids were not the least bit interested but, as parents, we felt that they would gain some insight and understanding of the country they left behind.

Kartya had a strong love of Chinese food at a very early age. Othmar would buy Chinese sausages for himself because no-one else liked them. He would give one to Kartya and she would demolish it in five minutes. She would dip it in soy sauce and suck the sauce off. She loved rice, noodles and spring rolls. Kiersten on the other hand hated Chinese food. She once said to me, 'Mum, I'm Asian and I don't like Asian food, how come?' I said, 'Well, you're only half Asian. Maybe that's why.' We did look an interesting bunch of people. When we all went out together, we would get some very strange looks.

CHAPTER SIX

Romduol and Heng

It was in March 1982 that we heard through a friend who was a social worker about two Cambodian sisters who were living in a migrant hostel in Springvale. The hostel was interim accommodation for refugees from other countries. They usually stayed two months until they were able to find somewhere else to live. The sisters had escaped from the horror created by the Pol Pot regime and fled to resettlement camps in Thailand. Othmar and I went to visit them, to see if we could do anything to help them. The girls were quite fascinated with Kiersten and Kartya. I think they thought it was unusual for us to have adopted two little girls. Our first impression of Romduol, 21, and Heng, 19, was that they were beautiful, gentle young ladies.

Their main concern was that they had no accommodation to move into after leaving the hostel. They needed to vacate their small, pokey little room, to make way for someone else to move in. When they told us of their enormous struggle to survive their journey from Cambodia to Australia, we wanted to help them. We asked them if they would like to come and live with our family, until something more permanent could be organised. So our family expanded by two more members.

We all fell in love with Romduol and Heng. They quickly became part of our family. We all loved having them around, especially the kids. The girls told them all sorts of interesting stories about their life in Cambodia. They came from a world and culture that we had only ever read about in the newspapers.

Kartya became their cherished child. She was always getting carried around on someone's hip. Her strong-willed antics earned her the nickname 'the monster'. If she didn't get her own way, she would stand in the one spot and stamp her feet and hold her breath until her face was so red she looked like she would explode. I don't think Romduol and Heng had seen anything like that; they were so quiet and gentle.

After several weeks, we asked them if they would like to stay with us indefinitely. We were all a bit squashed, but we adjusted to the extra members of our family and they added a different dimension to our family unit. We wanted to be able to help them and supported their desire to resume their education, which had been disrupted. Their father had been a teacher and they told us that it would have been his wish for them to have a good education.

The girls would help me to feed and bath the kids. They also looked after them at night while Othmar and I were working in our restaurant. Their help and loving care was invaluable to us. They would cook us some interesting meals, too, such as Heng's special fried rice or spring rolls with all sorts of vegetables in them. I would teach them to cook some European meals and my favourite chicken vegetable soup.

44

Someone always had to keep an eye on Kartya. We would all take turns: me, Othmar, Romduol and Heng. The minute you took your eyes off her, she would disappear. Once we found her under the house, lying on her tummy, trying to pull the cat out by the tail. Poor Snowy was meowing and writhing around, but Kartya would not let go. She gave the poor cat hell. Every time Snowy walked past her, she would grab his tail. In the end we couldn't coax that cat out from under the house.

Every Monday night would be swimming lessons. Come rain, hail or shine, we would all take Kiersten, Alex and Josh off to the swimming pool. I never learnt to swim and nearly drowned as a child, so I was determined that our kids would swim. Kartya would come along as an interested observer. She was too young to start lessons. One night, Othmar was standing on the edge of the pool, holding her hand. Next we knew, she pulled her hand out of Othmar's and jumped in the water. I screamed. Othmar jumped in, fully clothed. She was in the water, bobbing up and down like a cork, with this big smile on her face. He dragged her out, but she wanted to go back in. She had no fear at all. Kartya feared nothing. The next week we got special permission to enrol her for lessons on the condition that I got in the water with her. She wasn't too thrilled about that because she wanted to swim on her own; she didn't want me holding her. She was unsinkable, our Kartya.

Romduol and Heng enrolled in a vocational course at Dandenong TAFE college. It taught them basic skills such as typing and general office skills that would give them better job prospects. They had already completed an English language course at the migrant hostel. Living with us made it easier because they were forced to speak English all the time. We all had some very funny times with pronunciation of words, me with my Aussie accent and Othmar with his German accent. It must have been quite confusing for the girls at times.

Every morning I would drive Romduol and Heng to the bus stop, Kiersten to school and Alex to kindergarten. I would then have all day to spend with Josh and Kartya. I would get organised first thing and prepare the meal for the evening. Sometimes we would go to the park and Josh and Kartya would play. After lunch they always went for a sleep. Josh would sleep but Kartya rarely did. She would look at her books or play with her favourite teddy and call out to me every five minutes, wanting to get up. She always had to be doing something: usually getting into some kind of mischief.

One morning I was in the kitchen, making homemade broth and putting it into little ice-cube trays. I made all the kids' food. Nothing frozen or takeaway. I thought Kartya was in the loungeroom with Josh building Lego. I heard Kartya scream, then she came running down the hallway with her mouth open, pointing inside it. I looked inside and couldn't see anything, but her mouth smelt funny. I went to the lounge and Josh said that she had gone into Romduol and Heng's room. I went in and on the floor was an empty pill container. On it was printed CHLOROPHYL TABLETS. I didn't have a clue what they were for, or how many had been in the container. I picked Kartya up, screaming, grabbed Josh by the hand and raced over the road to our family doctor. He said that the pills were anti-malaria tablets and were highly dangerous. He gave Kartya some syrup to make her sick. She vomited up six tablets. The doctor couldn't be sure how many she had ingested, so he rang an ambulance and off we went to hospital—back to the same one she had been in as a baby. They pumped her stomach and ascertained that she had swallowed approximately thirty tablets. Enough to kill her. They kept her in hospital for twenty-four hours, under observation. On her medical chart at the end of her bed, it read:

Two-year-old girl, very fit-looking, playing with toys, responsive, not at all sick-looking. No obvious effects from overdose on Chlorophyl tablets.

Othmar and I were stunned. We could have lost her: but this tough little kid kept bouncing back no matter what happened to her.

Poor Romduol and Heng felt so guilty. They had been given the tablets when they were in the camp in Thailand. We didn't blame them; after all, Kartya had to climb onto a bed, then up onto a fireplace overmantel, nearly up to the ceiling, to even reach them. We obviously had a budding gymnast on our hands. From then on, I would get very nervy when she was out of my sight.

Kiersten, Alex and Josh loved to play with Kartya when she was in her good mood. She could be a happy little thing, squealing with delight as they chased her around and around the house. Kiersten would read her stories at night; Kartya always wanted the same one read over and over.

Mornings were a huge production with everyone getting ready to go to their various destinations. We only had one toilet inside the small bathroom, so it was a bit like an army camp to accommodate everyone. One morning Kartya was eating her breakfast; the next minute she was gone. We couldn't find her anywhere. The other kids were outside looking for her; Othmar and I were up and down the street. Romduol and Heng were at the neighbours. Nobody could find Kartya. I was freaking out. Othmar found her around at the corner shop, sitting on the step, waiting for it to open. He was dragging her back and she was screaming, 'Mum, icy pole. Icy pole.' We were all so relieved. I thought she'd been kidnapped. From then on, there was an unspoken agreement: don't let this kid out of your sight.

As Romduol and Heng became more comfortable with our family, they told us of their incredible journey. They had been imprisoned by Pol Pot's regime in Kampuchea and forced to work in the rice paddies for fifteen hours a day, like most people in those days living under totalitarian rule. Children as young as ten were separated from their parents and taken away to work. Romduol and Heng became very depressed, disillusioned and physically exhausted from the hard work and lack of food. They watched people around them drop dead like flies from starvation and diarrhoea. They saw many people executed before their eyes. Their mother and father, from whom they had been separated, died of starvation. A week later they heard that their baby sister and seven-year-old brother had also died from starvation. They were not allowed to go back to their village to see their parents either when they were ill or when they had died. Despite their overwhelming sadness and physical weakness they remained mentally strong, hoping for the day when they would be freed from the evil regime. Unable to wash their hair for four years, they rubbed lemon on their skin and in their hair to smell fresh.

After nearly four years, the Pol Pot regime was driven out by military force to the border by the Vietnamese troops that invaded Cambodia in late 1978. When this happened, people lived in fear of the new Vietnamese-backed government. Feeling very heavy-hearted, Romduol and Heng decided to leave their beloved country. They left on foot, walking more than one hundred kilometres to the Thai–Cambodia border, walking through the jungle littered with minefields and swimming across rivers, always in fear of being captured by the Vietnamese guards.

When they reached the Thai–Cambodia border they stayed at a refugee camp for about a month, but did not feel at all safe as there was a lot of fighting every day between the Khmer Rouge rebels and other faction groups. One day, news came to them that new refugee camps had been built inside Thailand and were ready to receive refugees. The United Nations High Commission for Refugees organised buses to transport people to the new camps. Romduol and Heng were provided with water, food and cooking utensils. They made a life for themselves along with other refugees and stayed there for eighteen months awaiting sponsorship by a relative in Melbourne, so they could start a new life.

Othmar and I admired the courage and strength with which they overcame the immense pain and hardships that they had endured. They were not at all bitter, rather they were grateful that they were able to begin a new life in Australia. We felt that the least we could do was support and love them. We embraced both girls as part of our family.

Three months later, Romduol received news that a younger brother and sister were still alive and living in another refugee camp in Thailand. They immediately made contact and began sponsorship proceedings in order to be reunited with them in Australia.

When we heard the news, I was ecstatic, jumping all over the place. Romduol and Heng were more reserved, but were quietly excited. I said to them straight away, 'They can live here, with us.' I assured the girls that we would do whatever we could to help. When Othmar got home from work that night, I told him what had happened and he said, without reservation, 'They'll live here, won't they?' Romduol told us that their sister, Sophea, was sixteen and brother, Vichea, was fifteen. I thought to myself, what the heck, two more is not going to make that much difference. After all I'm one of ten. But I wished we had another bathroom and toilet.

After months of waiting, finally Sophea and Vichea arrived. We all went to the airport to meet them. They both looked very thin and frail, and very sad. They were so young and yet had been through so much. Sophea was beautiful, with long black hair down her back. Vichea was a handsome young boy and so very shy. He looked totally lost.

We took them home to Vermont, to our big rambling weatherboard house that was now bursting at the seams. It must have been such a culture shock for them both. We showed Vichea and Sophea around the house, explaining how all the modern conveniences worked. It was such a big adjustment for them. They had not seen their two sisters for six years, so they had to renew family relationships as well as try to fit in to this rather odd family.

I think that our four little children played an important part in the re-bonding process of this family that had been ripped apart by a war. All the kids wanted to be part of Romduol, Heng, Sophea and Vichea's lives. They would talk to them, sing to them, play with them and, at times, drive them nuts. Sophea and Vichea showed love and affection for the little ones and I'm sure that helped to take away some of their pain. Considering we suddenly had eight children in the family, things progressed quite smoothly. Romduol, Heng, Vichea and Sophea gave us much more than we could have ever given them back. They helped us with the running of the house in every way they could. Everyone did their share; the girls would help with the cooking, and every Saturday would be cleaning day. Everything got washed and scrubbed; it was amazing how organised we were.

We would all sit up until late at night, and they would tell us their stories. They felt that their parents were watching over them. Romduol told us that their father was a very kind and gentle man; very serious and hardworking, a man who had always wanted his children to have a good education and do well in society. Their parents would have been proud of them.

Sophea and Vichea commenced language school and began to learn a new language and a new lifestyle. They were very happy days for all of us. Our friends were very supportive of our commitment to help others and they helped us wherever they could. Most of them were adoptive parents and had been supportive of us over the years.

I suppose Othmar and I were a bit like foster parents in a way. We tried to help with schoolwork and we were very proud of our extended family's achievements. The four of them would sit up at the dining room table until all hours of the morning, doing homework and studying. They were so committed. We often hoped that our four kids would follow their example.

Vichea was a wonderful artist and he would do some beautiful, but sad, drawings of his life in the camp in Thailand.

One day one of the kids came home with head lice. It was a nightmare. Everyone had these little things crawling in their hair and, as all the girls had this thick, long waist-length hair, we had to get dozens of bottles of solution from the council to wash everyone's hair in. We had to wash all the bedding every day for weeks to get rid of the pests. I suggested that everyone get their hair shaved off, but no-one was too enthusiastic about that suggestion. The house smelt like the local pharmacy. It was quite a production, washing and combing everyone's hair every night, in one little bathroom.

When the time came for our extended family to move on, we were all very sad. We didn't want them to go, but we knew they had to. They had to establish their own family unit. We were all to miss them very much.

CHAPTER SEVEN

A Seed of Doubt

ome nights I would go to work in our restaurant named 'The Spit', that we owned in partnership with our friends Pat and Oscar. It was a big two-storey building with seating for one hundred and fifty people. The menu consisted mainly of French and Italian food. The specialty on the menu was a hot seafood salad, courtesy of a crazy Polynesian chef we had employed who would keep losing his temper and walking out on us at the drop of a hat, leaving Oscar to cook for the night. Othmar and Oscar worked every day, lunch and dinner. We all loved Pat and Oscar because they had introduced us to Kartya with that first baby photo. We felt quite a bond with them. Their baby Sharn was also adopted from Taiwan. She was the much-loved sister of Sioni, adopted by Pat and Oscar from the Philippines.

One Saturday night at about 12 o'clock we were just about to close the restaurant door and go home. The phone rang and Pat answered it. 'It's some guy with an accent wanting Mrs Wunderle,' she said. I took the phone thinking it may have been one of Othmar's relatives from Germany. It wasn't. It was a journalist from the *United Daily* newspaper in Taipei. He asked me what I thought about the fact that the lawyer who had handled Kartya's adoption for us had been charged with offences regarding illegal adoption of children to overseas countries.

I was speechless. My heart was thumping. I told him that I didn't know what he was talking about. I told him that we had heard nothing about it in Australia and, as far as I was concerned, we had done a perfectly legal adoption. He asked me what I thought about the Taiwanese government's plan to try and bring the children back to Taiwan. I was suddenly terrified that we had done something wrong; that someone would come and take Kartya away from us. The journalist suddenly changed tack and assured me that our papers were in order. He said it appeared that Kartya's birth mother, Lin-Ah-Hua, had willingly given Kartya up for adoption because she was poor and unable to care for her. I asked him how he got my phone number, and he said, 'Oh, very easy. You only Wunderle in Australia.'

Pat was standing beside me. I got off the phone and we hugged each other: They had adopted Sharn through the same so-called lawyer. What does this mean? we thought. What about our kids? Where does this leave us? We told Othmar and Oscar and they were both gobsmacked.

Several days later the story was all over the papers. Headlines read: INTERPOL TO HELP STOLEN BABIES' NATURAL PARENTS and TAIWAN BABY ADOPTION RACKET ERUPTS and 45 DETAINED OVER BABY TRADE RACKET.

Othmar and I felt sick with worry. What if something had been done illegally? What if Kartya's birth mother had not given her up? All sorts of things went through our minds. We couldn't eat, we couldn't sleep. All we could do was wait and see—wait until someone contacted us officially. We contacted a lawyer to try and understand our rights. She looked at our adoption papers and assured us that they were all in order and legal. The only thing that would render them illegal, she said, was if Kartya had been stolen from her mother. We prayed that was not the case. Meanwhile we had newspapers from Taiwan and Australia contacting us for information. All I could say was no comment because we had done what we thought was a normal overseas adoption. We had paid the legal fees, court costs, document translations and nursery fees. Although, considering the condition she was in when she arrived, the nursery fees were suspect. Altogether it was around $2000 Australian—not a huge amount in our eyes. It had not been much less for Kiersten's adoption a few years before.

From the newspaper reports, it appeared in some cases the birth mother's consent to adoption had not been given. One report in the Melbourne *Age* said, 'Several of the infants that had been investigated had been illegally adopted and had been sold without the consent of the birth mothers.'

Taiwanese authorities and Interpol launched a massive investigation into the activities of the Taipei-based ring and they found that obstetricians, lawyers and midwives, were all babysitters involved in buying and selling infants for adoption abroad. Investigators were looking at the circumstances surrounding the adoption of sixty-four infants living in Europe, America and Australia. Julie Chu, the lawyer, *our* lawyer, was revealed as a law clerk who posed as a lawyer. She reportedly told Taiwanese police she was doing charity work to 'find a happier environment for unhappy children'. We never heard from any official authority telling us anything, so we assumed that Kartya's adoption was not under scrutiny. It never occurred to us to confirm that LinAh-Hua was Kartya's birth mother. We simply believed the information on her adoption papers.

Pat and Oscar never heard anything either. Sharn continued to live happily with her Australian family oblivious to the anguish her parents were experiencing. We all believed that if the birth mothers had not consented, then one of them—or a relative—could have easily identified the children. Interpol had photographs of the babies and they had been widely distributed to the press. When we heard nothing, we were relieved. Enough tears had been shed and enough nights had passed without any sleep. We needed to put it behind us.

That whole episode cemented my love for Kartya. I would look at her and feel a surge of emotion. Nothing was ever going to affect my love for her. Othmar and I decided then that one day when Kartya was old enough we would find her birth mother and tell her how much we cared about her baby; the baby that for some reason she was unable to care for herself. We were the 'caretakers' and we would do the very best that we could; we would never waver from that commitment.

CHAPTER EIGHT

An Independent Child

Sundays were always a special day for our family. It was the one day of the week that Othmar was at home so we always went out for the day. We would load the cricket bats, footballs and a barbecue lunch and head for the hills to our favourite destination, Silvan Dam. It was a huge park with rolling hills, walking tracks and barbecues, and lots and lots of people. We would get there early to choose our own rotunda. The kids loved it, especially Kartya. She could run for miles, free. No matter how far she went, I could always see her. It was the one time that Othmar and I could sit, relax, talk and not worry about things.

Kartya was always happier playing on her own. She would roll down the hills on her side, right down to the bottom. She'd get up, grass all over her, face as red as a beetroot, run back up to the top and roll all the way down again. Her energy was a bottomless pit. I would run down to her, scoop her up in my arms and she'd fight to get free. I'd brush her down and she'd push my hands away, and say, 'Mummy, I can brush myself.' I'd think to myself, Isn't there anything I can do for you? You don't have to do everything for yourself.

She didn't mind Kiersten carrying her around. She seemed to relate to her and would let her do anything for her. Sometimes she would get Kiersten to dress her, but when it came to doing up buttons, Kiersten would ask me to do it. She couldn't stand to touch buttons. Once, just to upset her, the boys put buttons in her bed. Alex, especially, liked playing tricks on the girls. He would put these funny masks on, pop out of nowhere and frighten the living daylights out of them. Kartya loved it, she would shriek for more. Kiersten, on the other hand, was not impressed. She would get scared and become very upset with him.

When Kartya was about three, I was given the opportunity to work part time, from 10 a.m. until 2 p.m. three days a week. I thought that it would be good for me to get out of the house. Besides, with Kiersten, Alex and Josh all at school, Kartya was bored. She didn't seem too excited about spending all day with me. And the extra money would come in handy; we certainly needed it.

We had a very good friend who was in charge of a residential daycare centre, about a ten-minute drive from our home. She was an adoptive parent with two children from Vietnam. I asked her if she would care for Kartya on the days that I had to work. She said that she would be delighted to. It was a huge old rambling brick building, with lots of rooms and a big open kitchen. The outside area had heaps of playground equipment. I knew this would be wonderful for Kartya and that she would love climbing up on all these contraptions.

There were about twenty children in care at any one time and plenty of staff to watch over them. Some of the children were in short-term foster care, so they slept overnight. It was a bright, happy environment. I had no doubt it would be good for Kartya.

Perhaps she would learn to play with the other kids, rather than always preferring to play on her own.

I explained to Kartya that she was going to her own kindergarten. She was very excited about it. I explained to the staff that Kartya was very strong-willed, not at all compliant, and that she had a habit of screaming and holding her breath. I would take her there on my way to work and pick her up on my way home. She loved it from the beginning and didn't mind going at all. I would take her into the big kitchen and give her a hug—unreciprocated, of course. She would look at me as if to say, 'Bye. Make sure you don't come back too soon.'

She never wanted to come home with me when I went to pick her up. I would walk out the back to the big playground and call her name. She would look up at me, then turn around and continue playing. All the other kids would run into their mum's arms. Not Kartya. She would be angry because I had interrupted her play. She would start to stamp her feet and hold her breath. I would sweep her up into my arms and kiss her on the face. Her legs would be thrashing about and she'd be screaming, 'Mum, I want to stay, I don't want to go home.' I would strap her in the car seat and off we'd go. By the time we were at the first set of traffic lights, she'd be kicking the back of my seat with such force that I'd be squashed up against the steering wheel. She'd be screaming, 'Mum, I want to get out. Let me out.' By the time we drove into the driveway at home her face would be ready to explode. I would undo her seat belt and she would nearly fall out of the car. She didn't like being restricted in movement one bit, not one bit. She would react as if you were trying to kill her.

Every day she went to her kindergarten we would go through this torture.

After about three months my friend, the head of the centre, called me aside and said, 'I think your daughter has a few problems.' I jokingly replied, 'Yes, I know. Her name's Kartya.' We both laughed. Kartya had been displaying antisocial behaviour by being overly aggressive to the other kids. She would not do what she was told and would scream the place down and hold her breath. They had also noticed her lack of affection towards me. She told me that she had a friend who had adopted two children from an orphanage in Vietnam and had encountered similar experiences with them: the inability to give or receive affection, the anger, the detachment. She told me that this friend had been to a clinic in America, run by a man named Foster Cline. He specialised in treatment of children affected by abandonment issues. His diagnosis of these kids was that they were suffering from a condition he called 'lack of attachment'.

My friend believed that Kartya displayed the classic symptoms of this disorder. We knew that Kartya had some sort of symptoms but of what, we were not sure. She gave me a book to read called *Parenting With Love & Logic* that Foster Cline had written. After reading it, I had no doubt that Kartya was affected by the disorder. The anger, detachment, lack of interest in displays of love and her food fetish all pointed to a lack of trust towards anyone.

The mother of the two Vietnamese orphans had taken one of her children to America and had been through a treatment program called Holding Therapy in which two people held the child and restricted them in movement. The idea was the child worked through their anger and eventually became subdued. Through this they learnt love and trust. This mother had learnt to conduct the treatment program herself, so my friend asked me if we would like to participate in the program with Kartya. I spoke to Othmar, and we decided that it might help Kartya. We made arrangements to take her to the centre the next evening at 7 p.m.

We met the adoptive mother and she explained the procedure to us. She also showed us a certificate to say that she was trained in Holding Therapy. She told us how beneficial it had been for her son, and that he was now a different person, able to give and receive love and affection. We liked her and felt very confident in her ability. After all, it couldn't do any harm.

The two women took Kartya off and told us that it could take several hours. Othmar and I sat in the reception area and watched television and waited. About two hours later they returned. My friend was holding Kartya in her arms. She handed her to me and she snuggled into my chest. I wrapped my arms around her and held her close. She allowed me to cuddle and kiss her. Her face was bright red, but she was very calm and submissive. Othmar took her and held her. She looked almost happy. They told us that she had become very angry when held down. They felt that the procedure had been very successful. We would need to take Kartya for at least ten more treatments until she learned the love and trust necessary to overcome her anger, they said. We thanked them and left. All the way home in the car, she snuggled into me; she seemed exhausted. It was the first time that I had felt her respond to affection. The next day she seemed quite subdued, very quiet, not at all like the Kartya we were used to. I had second thoughts about the treatment. It had changed her. I didn't want to go ahead with it any more.

Othmar and I discussed it, and he thought that before continuing with it, we should take her to a specialist in child behaviour. I got a referral from our family doctor who thought I was being a bit anxious and overprotective. He thought Kartya was 'as tough as old boots'. In time, he said, she'd be all right; she just had a bad temper.

Othmar and I took Kartya along to the specialist. His office was situated in a big bluestone building in one of the better streets in the city. We were ushered into his office by a matronly looking lady with thick-framed black spectacles. We met Dr Michael Darebin. He was an elderly gentleman with balding grey hair, dressed in a grey flannel suit and white shirt and tie. He looked very professional. I thought he looked a bit like Dr Spock. Othmar and I sat down. I had Kartya sitting on my knee and she kept kicking his desk with her foot. We described Kartya's behaviour to the doctor. We mentioned that we thought she might have been suffering from a lack of attachment. He said that was a lot of 'poppycock'. He didn't believe in labelling kids because of their behaviour. 'She looks normal to me,' he said.

He said that it was normal for the baby of the family to want their own way all the time. I asked about the fact that she hated to be cuddled or held. He said, 'Don't worry about it. If she wants to be loved she'll come to you. Obviously she doesn't need it.' We thought that was a bit strange; we were all warm, loving, caring people. Kiersten, Alex and Joshua loved to be cuddled. We loved to cuddle them, so why didn't Kartya like it?

We went home, determined to continue to engage Kartya in the affectionate behaviour that was the core of our family existence. Sometimes I would put my hands on Kartya's cheeks when I talked to her, to encourage her to look at me. I would say to her, 'Look at me, Kartya.' She would never look at me; her head and eyes would be darting all over the place. Not just with me; with everyone. It was hard to engage eye contact with her. When I thought I had succeeded, she would screw her face up. Her eyes would disappear and she would say 'Mummy, you can't see me. I don't want you to see me.'

I always believed the eyes were the mirror to the soul. I wasn't going to see her soul, that's for sure. One day when I was at the doctor's I mentioned it to him. He said, 'Oh, that's nothing unusual. Some adults won't look you in the eye, that doesn't mean anything.'

I started to think that maybe I was becoming a bit obsessed with Kartya's behaviour. It was just that I wanted her to be happy, to be able to feel that she was part of the family, that she fitted in somewhere. She had such a likeable personality, with this fiercely independent nature and the most wicked guttural laugh; that we'd ever heard. I liked it when I would hear her laugh; it made me think she was happy.

It was at kindergarten that Kartya started to relate and play with other kids. Othmar and I would take turns to take her there. She always wanted one of us to stay and cut up the fruit. That was a promising sign: she wanted us to be with her. At playtime, I would find her climbing up the playground equipment to the top and then she'd hang mid-air with the blood running to her head and she'd scream, 'Mummy, catch me.' She still had no fear.

She did love to play with the other kids, but there were conditions attached. She had to be the boss. If she didn't get her own way, she would walk off and play on her own. Her paintings were a work of art. She loved to paint. She would use every colour in the pots. If it wasn't going the way she wanted, she would turn the pot of paint upside down on the floor. Paint would run everywhere.

She made lots of friends at kindergarten. She was always inviting kids home to sleep the night. I wouldn't know about it until some mother would ring me up and thank me for inviting their child to stay. She certainly was a gifted child at organising her social life. When they had story time at kinder, all the kids would sit on a mat on the floor. Kartya would squat. She hardly ever sat down. Even when she watched television at home, she squatted in front of it. She would sometimes eat squatting on the floor. I would look at her and smile and shake my head. I would think, you are such a funny little girl, you've never seen anyone squat and yet you do it as if it's second nature.

I always had to pack her a kinder lunch. Half the time she didn't eat it, she would just bring it home and store it in her room. She would say to me, 'Mum, I need it in case I get hungry.' The first thing she did when she walked in the door from kinder was to open the refrigerator door and say, 'Mum, what can I have to eat?'

Her favourite game at home with the other kids was mothers and fathers. She always had to play the mother—if she couldn't, she wouldn't play. Kiersten, Alex and Josh accepted her pushy personality. Her interpretation of a mother was to run around with the wooden spoon smacking them on the bottom. They would always ask her what game she wanted to play. She always had first choice. They would beg her to play the game of pressing her face against the window. Kartya would go outside the window and press her face up against it until it was as flat as a pancake. She would look such a sight. They would be falling all over the place laughing hysterically and the more they laughed, the longer she did it.

Out of everyone in the family, her favourite person remained Othmar. She interacted with him easily. She preferred men. She befriended every man who was part of our family. I once said to Othmar, 'I bet if I was a man, she'd like me.' She would beg Othmar to give her 'the treatment'. The treatment was rubbing his beard over her face. She would scream with delight. He would chase the kids all over the house, calling out, 'Who wants the treatment?' Kartya would be calling, 'Me, daddy. Me first.'

From the other kids she got the nickname 'Daddy's little darling, Mummy's little nightmare'. Once when Kartya kicked me in the shins for something that I probably didn't do, Kiersten said, 'Mum, why is Kartya so mean to you?' I said to her, 'I don't think she means it, she just gets angry. She'll grow out of it.' Kiersten replied, 'It can't be because she's adopted. I'm adopted too and I'm not angry with you.' No, she wasn't angry. Kiersten was never angry with anyone, it wasn't in her nature. Her personality was serene and peaceful. The girls were so opposite; maybe that's why they got on well together.

CHAPTER NINE
Unreal Mother

We were still working hard in our restaurant, but business was not always kind to us. We would have few people midweek and on Friday and Saturday night we would be packed with about 120 people. Still, it was not enough to sustain two families. Sadly, we decided with Pat and Oscar to sell it. After months of trying, we eventually found a buyer. We both lost a lot of money. We had to sell our lovely old home in Vermont and move. We bought a cheaper house about ten minutes away in Mitcham Road. So off we went. Packed everything up and said goodbye to the house we all loved. Left it for some other family to enjoy. I would drive past sometimes just to look at it and check that the garden was being watered. I found it hard to let go. One day when I drove past, I saw our beautiful big chandelier sitting on the nature strip as destructible garbage. I was mortified. I went up and knocked on the front door of my old house and asked the owners if I could take it home. They were happy to let me have it. So I loaded my chandelier into the car and took it home to Mitcham Road. Obviously the new owners didn't like my crystal lights as much as we did. They didn't like the way I had decorated it either because they had pulled the wallpaper off the walls and painted them all a dull grey. After seeing that, I didn't miss the house any more.

Our house on Mitcham Road was a huge old two-storey weatherboard painted mission brown. From the outside it didn't look all that flash. It had lots of rooms and two bungalows out in the back garden. It was on a large block with plenty of room for the kids to play. It needed a lot of work, but it had loads of potential. When I first saw the house, I walked in the front door and said straight away to the real estate agent, 'I'll have it'. I rang Othmar at work and said, 'Guess what? We just bought a house.' He always trusted my judgement. I knew he would like it.

The kids chose their own rooms. Alex and Josh shared a room. They had bunk beds and wanted to share. Kiersten had a lovely room overlooking the back garden. Kartya chose the room with windows opening on to the balcony. We decided to wallpaper the girls' rooms first. Othmar and I took them to the wallpaper shop to choose their own paper. Kiersten chose a white paper, with little pink flowers over it. It suited her personality. Soft, pretty, tranquil. Kartya chose bright, fiery Chinese red with little blue flowers on it. It suited her: bold and overpowering. They loved helping us decorate their rooms. When the girls' rooms were finished, we started on the rest of the house. One night when I was in the girls' rooms tucking them in, I looked at Kartya asleep in bed. Her big fat red cheeks matched her wallpaper. I thought what a good choice she had made, although I wasn't too sure that it would help her anger problem. Waking up in a red, fiery room wouldn't be conducive to a relaxed start to the day.

Kiersten, meanwhile, was asleep in her pretty tranquil relaxed room. Our two daughters, like chalk and cheese, both so precious. We were grateful for every day with them.

Every night when Othmar came home from work at about midnight, he would always go in and check on the kids, one by one. Every night, without fail. They all knew that they had a wonderful father. They absolutely adored him. He always made time for his kids. He never fobbed them off. If they ever wanted to know anything, he would take the time to explain things to them. He would say, 'All right, get yourself a drink. Sit down and I will tell you the whole story.' And he always did.

From a very early age, both our girls had their adoption papers. Kartya had a big folder and written on the outside in black texta it said: 'Kartya's Adoption Papers'. We kept the originals and photocopied all the documents. Kiersten never bothered all that much with hers. Kartya, on the other hand, would keep them in her room. Sometimes we would look at them together; other times I would find them strewn around her room, where she had been perusing them herself. I explained to her who Lin-Ah-Hua was and that, judging by her adoption papers, she was the same age as me. The papers stated that Kartya was the third daughter, so we assumed that she had two older sisters. Her birth father was not listed. She never asked about him. She wasn't interested in a father. She only ever mentioned her mother. We told her that one day, if she wanted, we would try and find her.

Kiersten always knew that we would not be able to find her birth family. She knew her papers were fake. Othmar had told her the story of going to the orphanage in Saigon to adopt her. The priest had flicked through a pile of birth certificates of babies who had died. He picked one out that matched as closely as possible to her age and that became a passport to her new life. She always knew these facts and so it never bothered her. She knew that without that piece of paper she would not have been able to leave the country. She never talked about a birth mother. The priest told Othmar the story of Kiersten's two aunties, aged about thirteen and fifteen, taking Kiersten to the orphanage because her birth mother had gone away and had not returned. The two young girls were unable to care for Kiersten any longer. We believed that her mother was Vietnamese and that her father may have been American. She was not full Vietnamese. At times she would wonder how she got her 'blue eye'. It was her birthmark. She was born with the white of one eye a deep blue. Once when I took her to an eye specialist to get new glasses, he said that it was very unusual. It was only found in Asians and Africans and then only rarely. It was genetic. She also had a 'bat ear': one ear stuck out. We thought it was unusual that both our girls had funny eyes and a birthmark around the eye.

We often wondered which family members our girls resembled. With a biological child, you can look at them and say he or she gets certain mannerisms from the father or the mother. With an adopted child, you can't do that. When they do strange things, you think, God, who do you get that from? The way Kartya would squat with such ease, as if it was second nature, intrigued us. When she would store food in her room, we would wonder why she did it. We fed her well, very well. It wasn't that she was hungry. It seemed to give her a sense of security. It was something she could control.

Kiersten had no such little foibles. She was happy and contented with her life. She had no complaints whatsoever. Considering they were all extremely different personalities, our four kids got on very well together. Whenever they did have fights, I would sit them down and make them apologise to each other. I would say to them,

'You must care about each other. You are brothers and sisters. You will always have each other to turn to.' They all understood. They knew that Othmar and I expected them to love each other. We tried very hard from the beginning to instil a sense of responsibility into each of them, a commitment to understand each other's feelings and an ability to accept each other no matter what.

It was always a big production getting them all ready for school in the mornings: breakfasts eaten, teeth cleaned, lunches made, bags packed and off to school. Kartya was always up first. She would get everything ready herself. Miss Independence never allowed anyone else to organise her. Her big achievement was to be allowed to walk to school on her own, with no big brother or sister to hold her hand. To her, it was freedom. In primary school, Kartya had lots of friends. She would boss them around and always make sure she got invited to someone's house after school to play.

Birthday parties for Kartya were a must. I'll never know how she did it, but she always got invited. Her name had to be on the list. Once she was getting ready to go to her friend Sandra's birthday party. I got out her pink denim overalls and a matching frilly pink shirt. She said to me, 'Mum, I don't want to wear those pants.' I said, 'Kartya, they look so pretty on you.' After much cajoling and bribery, she eventually decided to wear them. When I picked her up from the party, she was furious with me. 'Mum, I hate you. I'm never going to wear what you tell me ever again.' When I asked her why not, her answer was, 'I was the only girl wearing pants and I've had a terrible day.' Whenever she went to a party after that, she always wore a dress.

One of her best friends at primary school was a girl named Lisa. She was Chinese and Kartya liked her because she looked like her. She said once, 'Mum, I wish you looked like Lisa's mum.'

I replied, 'Kartya, no matter how hard you wish, there is no way I will ever look like Lisa's mum, but I'm sure your birth mother Lin-Ah-Hua does. One day we'll find her and you can see for yourself.' She was always very happy when I said that. We wanted her to feel that her birth mother was an important person, and that the door was always open for her to talk about it. Once, when I whacked her on the backside with the wooden spoon for writing over the newly painted wall with black texta, she yelled at me, 'I'm going to tell my real mother on you. Then you'll be sorry.' Kartya did not like discipline at all.

Academically, she was very clever. She had no problems with her school work at all. But the teachers told us that she was very disruptive in class. She distracted the other kids by always writing notes to them as she organised her social life. Whose house was she going to play at after school? Othmar and I both thought that somehow she coerced her little friends into inviting her to their house to play by telling them if they didn't invite her, then they couldn't come to our place. For some reason, unknown to us, they all loved coming to our house. Maybe it was the big rambling garden that they could run in, free to play hide and seek and climb the trees. I preferred to think that it was the afternoon tea parties that I would lay out on a table in the backyard.

Kartya would play cricket with Alex and Josh. They would get her to chase the ball, or find it when they had hit it into the bushes. At home, the four of them were always together playing. Sometimes Kartya would aggravate them when they wanted to watch television. She would do handstands in front of them and they couldn't see the show. Other times Alex would dink Kartya on the front of his bike. They would ride up and down Mitcham Road, with Kartya perched precariously on the handlebars. I would be out the front, screaming like a fishwife, 'Alex, come back! She'll fall off. Alex, come back, pleeeeease.' Kartya would tell me that I was a spoilsport. I was always a bit worried when Kartya and Alex would go off together because he was a bit of a daredevil and she didn't need all that much encouragement to get into mischief. The two of them would climb a big tree in the backyard. Kartya had to be up the top. I'd be freaking out. I would stand under the tree screaming at them, 'Kartya, come down this minute. You'll fall.' She would call out, pretending, 'Mum, I'm falling. I'm falling.'

Othmar and I decided to enrol her in gymnastics. We thought that we would channel some of her energy into a positive sport. Kiersten did calisthenics and she loved it, but Kartya didn't want to do that. She preferred the jumping, climbing, standing-on-the-head sports. She would get dressed in her tights and leotard and go off to the local high school gym. She wouldn't let me stay and watch her. She would tell me that I was embarrassing. When I asked her why, she once said, 'Mum, you're too bright and too pinky.' She was referring to the fact that my favourite colour is pink, bright pink, and I always wear bright pink lipstick. She continued by saying, 'Anyway, Mum, everyone knows you're not my real mum.'

One day I thought to myself, I'm getting a bit sick of hearing this, 'You're not my real mother' thing. I realised I was going to have to think of a positive way of dealing with it. I thought up the perfect solution. The opposite to real is unreal. That's it. I may not be the real mother, but there is nothing stopping me from being the 'unreal mother'.

I was to become the unreal mother of an absolutely unreal daughter. So it was that the unreal daughter continued going to gymnastics and learning new skills. Her favourite activity was to hang from the bars with blood running to her head and her long plaited pigtails swinging in the air. She delighted in showing her brothers and sister her new trick by hanging from the backyard tree upside down, with me standing below her, yelling, 'Kartya, get down. You're going to fall'. I was probably a bit overprotective of Kiersten and Kartya. More so than with the boys. I always felt that the boys would be all right: they knew who their mother and father was. With the girls I felt a responsibility and commitment that sometimes overwhelmed me. I wanted them to be able to deal with their adoption and be happy that we had adopted them.

CHAPTER TEN

Calm Before the Storm

~⌣~

I was working from home for a French skincare and cosmetic company. It suited us perfectly because I could be home during the day and when the kids got home from school. I would always have a treat ready for them as soon as they walked in the door. I would go out at night and demonstrate my products. We had a lovely neighbour who would come in and watch the kids until I got home. Her name was Doris. She lived alone in a unit across the road. She was about sixty and had grey hair dyed red. The kids said that her hair looked the colour of a carrot. Her warm, loving personality appealed to the kids and she would always bring them a delicious surprise to have before going to bed. My business was very successful and I made lots of friends. I achieved some overseas trips for my work, so Othmar and I had some nice times together without the kids. Kiersten, Alex and Josh usually stayed with friends while we were away. Kartya stayed with either my sister Nerida or our family doctor. He understood Kartya's personality and he was very firm with her. His wife and two daughters enjoyed having Kartya to stay. She loved it because they had a swimming pool in the backyard. One year she would stay at our doctor's, the next she would stay at Nerida's. They were the only two people who really understood Kartya and the only people who Othmar and I felt comfortable about leaving her with. She could be difficult but they were able to handle her without any drama. Kartya tried hard to control her Auntie Ned. Often the words 'You're not the boss of me, Auntie Ned' would spout from Kartya's perky little mouth. Whenever Auntie Ned or Uncle Nick challenged Kartya's behaviour she would want to ring Othmar and me in some faraway country and tell us. With a flat refusal from her auntie and uncle, she soon realised that perhaps for the time being they were the boss of her. Nerida would tell me that every night Kartya had to ring Kiersten, Alex or Josh, just to make sure that we hadn't come home and left her at Auntie Ned's under false pretences.

Her cousins, Anthony, Ben and Michael, were in awe at Kartya's physical dexterity when she was talking on the phone. She would climb up the door frame with feet and toes gripping either side of the door jamb, one hand holding the receiver and the other guiding herself up until her shoulders were pressing firmly on the top of the door frame. To walk through the door you had to walk under Kartya. Often she would ring Nerida and in her sweetest telephone voice, she would ask, 'Auntie Ned, can I come to your place to sleep?' Othmar and I would drive her over to their house and Kartya would join in the games with the boys. On a few occasions when she wasn't prepared to accept the house rules she would ring me up and say, 'Mum, come and get me, I hate this place.' I would go and get her and she'd be in a flood of tears, saying, 'I'm never coming back here ever again.' A month or so later, she'd ring Nerida. 'Auntie Ned, can I come for a holiday?'

We went to Thailand one year and on the way home we had a very rough flight. I was feeling bad enough as it was; I'd always suffered from a fear of flying, but I always felt more confident with fearless Othmar sitting beside me holding my sweaty hand. Flying didn't worry him at all. He told me to pretend that I was sitting in my favourite chair at home. As the plane hurtled through the air, falling hundreds of metres through the sky, I dug my nails into Othmar's wrist, and told him how scared I was. He looked at me with an ashen face and replied, 'So am I, love, so am I.'

I thought, if he's scared, this is serious. The girl behind us was sobbing hysterically and throwing up. It was the middle of the night, all the lights were off and there was no cabin staff to be seen. All I could think of was the beautiful amethyst ring that Othmar had bought for me on our American Express card. I had it on my finger and I was thinking how the kids were going to have to pay for it and it would be on my finger at the bottom of the ocean.

When we got back to Melbourne, I vowed and declared that I would *never* get on another plane. I felt like my whole life had flashed before my eyes. It made me realise how valuable my life was and how very precious Othmar and the kids were. They were my life, nothing was more important than them. I would nurture and protect them all forever. The realisation that we could have died gave me the inner strength to continue to face any obstacles that life would present.

We would often go and visit my mum and dad—Nanna and Pop to the kids. They loved to see how much the kids had grown.

Kiersten had a soft spot for her Nanna, she just loved her. Maybe it was because their personalities were so similar. They were both so soft and gentle and caring. Kiersten loved everyone in the family and so did Nanna. Nanna would call her 'my little Kiersten'.

Kartya's behaviour improved when she was about ten. At times she seemed to be a lot calmer and in control of her anger. She seemed to hate me less and talk to me more. I could sit down with her and talk about her life and she would look me in the eyes. One day I said to Pop, 'Pop, Kartya is a very good girl now.' He said, 'I've noticed she behaves better. Let's hope it lasts.' I replied, 'Of course it will, Pop, of course.'

Kartya started Girls Brigade at the church. It wasn't the normal church that we went to on special occasions, such as Christmas and Easter. Even though we didn't attend on a regular basis, religion was an important part of our lives, with Othmar often quoting passages of the Bible to the kids. Kartya would wear her little blue dress with the badges on it and put her hat on and walk up to the church clutching her Bible in her hands. They did all sorts of activities such as cooking, making up little books with religious stories in them, writing stories and sewing. She loved them all. I would stand at the front gate and watch her walk up the road to the church. When she got there, she would turn around and wave to me. At 9 p.m., Josh would ride his bike up to the church and walk her home. She would usually bring a piece of craftwork home that she had made for me.

She could be such a good girl. She still had her bad temper but she was really trying to keep it under control. When she felt like exploding, she would take herself off to her bedroom, removing herself from the rest of us. The other kids were very under. They knew that when she felt really angry about something, it was best to stay away from her and let her work through things on her own. She didn't want anyone to try and help her or talk to her, she just wanted to figure it out for herself.

When Kartya turned eleven she started lessons to make her first communion. Kiersten, Alex and Josh had all made theirs. Now it was her turn. She would go to church twice a week after school to prepare herself for her big day. We went to nearly every shop in Melbourne to try and find her a white communion dress. After much deliberation, she finally chose one. The big day arrived and we all went up to the church. We sat in the front row. The church was full. Our daughter was standing in front of the altar with seven other children. We were so proud of her. She looked like an angel standing there with the candle in her hand in her lovely white dress with the white headband holding back her shining black hair. After the ceremony, we all posed for photos. My favourite one shows Kartya sitting beside her dad, holding her communion certificate proudly in her hand. We all went home and had a special celebratory lunch.

This would be Kartya's last year of primary school before she moved on to secondary school. She wanted to do something with animals when she finished school. Othmar and I believed that she was smart enough to be a veterinary surgeon. Her marks at school were very good. We knew she should have no problems with the academic side of her education. However we were still a bit concerned about her social skills. Despite seeming to mellow as she approached adolescence, she occasionally relapsed into angry and aggressive behaviour. We seemed to cope with it well enough at home, but knew it wouldn't be tolerated in the high school environment. We were hoping that with her continuing maturity, she would grow out of it.

She had one really nice friend, Misty. She had been friends with Misty for a couple of years and we liked her a lot. They were total opposites, Kartya and Misty. Maybe that's why they were such good friends. Misty often stayed overnight with Kartya. She was quietly spoken, while Kartya was a bit of a loudmouth. We encouraged the friendship because Kartya appeared to be able to talk to Misty when she was unable to talk to us, her family, about her problems.

CHAPTER ELEVEN
Leaving Home

*D*uring the school holiday break of 1992 quite a few things changed in our family. Kiersten finished school and started working in a pharmacy. Alex commenced an apprenticeship as a hairdresser. Joshua was about to enter Year 9 and Kartya Year 7. It was during these holidays that Kartya started to go out with her friends and enjoy herself. She had lots of friends from primary school and Othmar and I knew them and their families.

Our kids had strict guidelines regarding the time that Othmar and I expected them home. Kiersten, Alex and Josh respected and abided by the rules. Kartya, however, could not stick to her commitment. She kept trying to push the boundaries further and further. I would drive her to her destination, make an arrangement to pick her up and she either would not be there or would refuse to come home with me.

I would get very frustrated and very angry. I would ground

her, only to find out that she had climbed out of her bedroom window. Othmar and I would then spend hours looking for her in the middle of the night. Sometimes we would find her walking the streets with a friend. We would bring her back home, but we were very worried about her because we could not talk to her. She would become very angry and aggressive and tell us that it was none of our business. She would threaten us that if we didn't let her do what she wanted, we would never see her again. She had us over a barrel and we often felt powerless to control her.

The other kids were not very impressed with her attitude towards me and Othmar and they would tell her so. She didn't care. She only cared about her friends. We hoped that the new year would be more positive and that with a new school and new challenges, Kartya would settle down and do what she could do best and that was to study hard for her future. At that stage it was not an unrealistic goal for us to look towards, and I couldn't wait to get her back to school and into a routine again.

The last few weeks of the holidays were taken up with buying new school books and uniforms for Kartya and Josh. Kartya seemed to be excited about the prospect of going back to school and diligently named all her belongings and covered her books with great precision. When the first day of the new school year arrived, Kartya got dressed in her new school uniform, her black shiny hair held in place with her customary headband, kissed me goodbye and went off on a new journey. As I watched her walk up the road, I said a silent prayer that she would stay there and not go climbing out of any windows. She looked so beautiful in her blue and white dress, long white socks and lace-up shoes.

I thought about her birth family and what they must look like. She must have got her tall stature from someone: her long feet, her wide shoulders, her beauty and her very bad temper. Othmar and

I had again, recently, discussed with her the possibility of trying to find her birth mother, Lin-Ah-Hua. We told her that when she felt the time was right, we would do everything to help her. She floated in and out of wanting to find her and not wanting to find her. She said to me, 'Mum, I don't want to find anyone that left me for dead and tied me up. What sort of mother would do that?' We tried to explain to her that until we knew the whole story, we had no right to judge. I told her that I believed her mother loved her. I had no doubt in my mind about that at all. We could only reassure Kartya that one day, when she was ready, we would discover her genetic background and unravel the mystery surrounding her adoption. When I found her adoption papers torn up, lying on the floor of her bedroom, I felt that day was not going to be too long in coming.

It was a chilly, overcast morning in March when I found myself sitting at the kitchen table in silence, unable to speak, almost unable to think. I didn't want to think, because if I did, I would have to try and understand why Kartya didn't want to live with us any more. Why did she go to the school counsellor and tell her that she didn't want to come home and live with us? Surely jumping out of her bedroom window at midnight, going off to God knows where, in the black of night, scaring the living daylights out of us, demanded some form of discipline? Othmar and I had grounded her. We said she couldn't go anywhere for a week. In return she mouthed at us every obscene word she could think up. I slapped her face. She glared at me and said, 'Mum, you'll be sorry.'

I received a phone call from the school. They said that I must come up to discuss a serious complaint that Kartya had made against us. When I arrived, the counsellor, a woman in her early forties, slim with short brown hair, said that Kartya had complained that she was being abused at home. I sat there thinking, What are you talking about? By who? I looked at Kartya sitting there in the red vinyl chair, her chin jutting out, her lips pursed, her head down in defiance and her long black shiny hair covering her face. 'Who is abusing you, Kartya?' I asked quite innocently. 'You, you bitch. You slapped my face,' she spat out at me. Then it hit me. That's what this is all about.

Then, in front of Kartya, the counsellor told me what I did was very bad for Kartya's self-esteem. Kartya had a smug look on her face, as if to say, 'See, you were wrong.' I felt like grabbing her by the ear and pulling her out of there. The counsellor suggested that maybe it would be best for Kartya to live somewhere else for a time—until we could get some family counselling to help us deal with the problem.

Kartya had a smile on her face. I was furious. I said that I didn't agree with this. Kartya said, 'Mum, I'm not coming home.'

How dare that teacher have suggested to her that it would be better that she live somewhere else for a time? This took all authority out of our hands. This gave Kartya control and this is what she wanted. Why couldn't the counsellor see this? What choice did we have? None. It was just not fair. Yes, she was hard to manage, hard to control and she was angry, aggressive and abusive. But we were doing our best and leaving home at twelve was not the answer.

I went home and rang Othmar at work. I told him what had happened. He said, 'We don't have to agree to that.' I tried to explain that I didn't think we had a choice; she didn't want to come home. At least, I said, she will be safe and we'll know where she is.

I told Kiersten, Alex and Josh that Kartya wouldn't be home that night. I was crying. They were more worried about me than about Kartya.

My friend Jan arrived. She gave me a hug and said she was sorry. She understood my pain, she was an adoptive parent herself. We had been friends for years, ever since she and Othmar came back from Vietnam together. Jan and her husband had adopted two children at the same time we adopted Kiersten. She came to give me support. We sat together at the kitchen table for hours. I was sobbing uncontrollably. Jan just sat and held my hand. I was shaking my head in disbelief. I felt like my world had fallen apart. The loss was indescribable. All I ever wanted to be was a good mother and now I felt like such a failure. I felt like someone had died. I felt like someone had cut me open and taken out my insides and put them all back in the wrong order. That's what it felt like.

Didn't she know how much we loved her? I told her once, 'Kartya, if you were really, really sick and you needed a new heart, then I would give you mine.' She said, 'But, Mum, then you would die.' I replied, 'Yes, that's how much I love you.'

Jan left. She assured me that it would all work out. She said that it was probably just a phase that Kartya was going through. I began to hope so. I began to think that maybe the next day Kartya would change her mind and come home where she belonged. I was sure she would miss us. I went to bed hoping to sleep the night away, praying that in the morning I would be able to go and get our daughter.

Sleep didn't come. I tossed and turned. I screamed inside my mind: Don't you know how much we love you? How can you be so cruel? Are we ever going to see you again? Othmar was sleeping soundly beside me. How could he sleep? I felt like putting a pillow over his head as he snored away. I got out of bed and went to the toilet and vomited.

Sleep came, eventually. I woke in the morning and my pillow was wet. Tears were still spilling out of my eyes. I made coffee and sat at the kitchen table opposite Othmar in silence. We couldn't speak. We were both fighting back tears.

I spoke with Kiersten, Alex and Josh. They couldn't understand why Kartya didn't want to live with them. I tried to reassure them that it would all work out.

I drove up to the railway station. I knew Kartya would be getting off the train to walk up to the school. I sat in my car for about ten minutes, then I could see her get off the train. I got out of my car, but I was afraid to approach her. She would only abuse me and run off. So I kept my distance. She met up with some friends and she was laughing and talking to them. I was hoping she would look unhappy, but she didn't look at all miserable. She looked happy. I followed her in my car all the way to school. She didn't see me. I returned home and tried to feel normal. In the afternoon, the school counsellor rang to tell me that she would come and pick up some of Kartya's clothes as she had decided to stay with the foster family for two weeks. Obviously Kartya didn't miss us at all.

I was unable to concentrate on anything. I felt a mixture of sadness and anger. I crawled into bed, taking my thumping head with me. I sandwiched it between two pillows but that didn't help much, just made the headache worse. Othmar rang me from work and said he couldn't concentrate on his job. He believed Kartya would come home that day. I didn't have the heart to tell him that she wouldn't be home for another two weeks. After school, Kartya and the counsellor arrived. I tried to talk to Kartya, but she wouldn't even look at me. She was very defensive. It was as if she was saying, 'Discipline me, and this is what I'll do to you.'

I said to her, 'Kartya, why? What have we done to you?' She just looked at me and said, 'You're not my real family. I can do what I want to do and you can't stop me.' She turned and walked out of the front door. In my heart I knew that things would never be the same again. I could see the anger she was feeling. The look in her eyes told me that deep inside her there was a lot of pain. I couldn't understand why a child that had been given so much love could appear to be in so much pain. It was almost as if she couldn't understand why she felt that way, and that the only way she could begin to deal with it was to remove herself from us.

She could see that I was a mess, and I knew that she would think about Othmar and know how he felt. She loved him, she always had. She must have been carrying a lot of guilt about what was happening to our family. I would ring her every night at the foster family's home, but she didn't want to talk to me. I would leave a message for her, to tell her that we loved her and wanted her back home. She never rang us back. She made it clear she wanted no contact with us whatsoever. We were hurt and we were sad and there was not a damn thing we could do about it.

Dreams

We try to help you
you just kick and scream
We bring you home
but it's all a dream
When we awake
you're still not there
We feel we failed
it's just not fair
We try our best
and we failed the test
I go to your room
and lay on your bed
on your pillow, I lay
my painful head
I go to sleep, and in my dream
I bring you home
but when I awake
you're still not there
It was all in my dreams.

CHAPTER TWELVE

The Dope Stuff

It took nearly a month for the school counsellor to organise counselling for our family. In that time, Kartya had come home, stayed two weeks, then packed her things and gone walkabout again. The whole family went to a local organisation that specialised in family conflicts. We were assigned a support worker to help us work through our problems. We didn't know who Kartya was staying with. She would just say 'a friend'. The support worker was in contact with Kartya and assured us that she was all right. She turned up at one session looking dishevelled, dirty and unkempt. Her beautiful long black hair was greasy and she looked very sad. She sat throughout the session with her head down, uncommunicative, unresponsive and aggressive.

After much negotiation, we came to an agreement that was typed up and signed by the whole family. Kartya would agree to attend school and if she was caught wagging more than twice in term four, we would look into the matter further and talk to the principal, or change schools. Kartya agreed to abide by the guidelines regarding going out. These remained as they had been before she left home: I would drive her and pick her up. Kartya agreed to go to a counsellor to learn how to deal with her anger and aggression. If her behaviour did not improve and the situation became intolerable for all concerned, then Human Services would be notified and they would take over the case.

It was very difficult for all of us. We all had to change to accommodate Kartya's needs. I couldn't help but wonder why she couldn't change for us. There were six of us in this family and five had to change for one. Wouldn't it be easier for one to change for five? We knew it didn't work that way, but we did hope and pray that it would all just get fixed and go away, then we could get on with our lives. We were all getting a bit tired of looking for Kartya every day. It was like hanging on to a tiger by the tail. Every time she would go walkabout, we would drag her back home again. I'd think to myself, how long will this go on? Surely not too much longer. I wanted my life back to some sort of normality; back to the times when I would tuck all of them into bed. Now I would go to Kartya's bed and half the time she was not even there.

Kartya went back to school and when she set her mind to it she came up with some really good work. Kiersten would help her with her homework when she needed it and the boys were very supportive of her. They just hated the fights and arguments, and Kartya and I fought nearly every day. It was always over discipline issues; her wanting to do something and me not allowing her. She would get very angry, stamp all the way upstairs to her room and start kicking the walls. Whenever we had a fight she would go into her bedroom, screaming, and you would hear her, lying on her bed kicking at the wall with her shoes on. I would tell her, 'Keep that up, and you'll have to pay to get it fixed.' She didn't care.

One night a friend of mine called in to pick something up. We were in the lounge room talking and we heard this thumping and banging. She said, 'What the hell is that?' I casually answered, 'Oh, that's Kartya. She's kicking holes in the wall.' She replied, 'If she was my child, I'd belt the living daylights out of her.' I tried to explain to her that wasn't the answer. It wouldn't make any difference. It would just make her angrier. I think my friend thought I was weak. She didn't understand that I had to be strong just to get through the day. No-one understood that.

Kartya continued to kick the walls in until nearly every wall had huge big holes, right through to the weatherboards. One day I got a tradesman in to give me a quote to fix the holes up. He went upstairs to assess the situation, came back down and said, 'With respect, Madam, how did that happen?' I said, 'My daughter has a bad temper.' He looked at me quizzically and said, 'Yeah, sure.'

I continually tried to talk to Kartya about her anger, but she wouldn't talk to me. I would tell her that I loved her, no matter what, and I would put my arms around her. She would stand as stiff as a board, with her arms by her side, unresponsive. It was like she was that tiny baby again and I was trying to hug an ironing board. She had built a brick wall around herself that no-one could penetrate, not even Othmar. Some days she would go to school, other days I couldn't get her out of bed. Then she would get ready to go to school and, somewhere along the way, get sidetracked and finish up on the other side of town.

One day, she just stopped going to school. She said, 'I'm not going back.' I said, 'You have to go to school. Everyone has to go to school, Kartya.' She was adamant. No-one was going to make her do what she didn't want to do, no matter what the consequences were. Othmar tried to talk to her. He usually had better luck than me, but this time his little pep talk fell on deaf ears.

She began to leave home for days on end and not come back. We were beside ourselves with worry. We approached several community organisations for help, but they all told us the same thing: if Kartya doesn't want to come home, then no-one can make her. On her behalf the school contacted an organisation that specialised in helping troubled adolescents. We were introduced to a young social worker called Lisa. Othmar and I both liked her and thought she would relate well to Kartya—if we could find her.

After a few days she turned up, in need of a shower and a decent meal. We asked her where she'd been and all she would say was with friends. We told her about Lisa and that we wanted to arrange a meeting with her. Kartya agreed. We met several days later at our home. Lisa wanted to know how she could help her. Kartya said that she didn't need help and that she could work things out for herself. Lisa told her that her expectations of her family were unrealistic and that if anything was to be resolved, Kartya had to agree to certain conditions regarding her future and education.

Kartya became very angry and told Lisa that it was none of her business. She stormed out of the house with me running after her, begging her to come back. She turned around, yelled, 'Fuck off,' and disappeared all the way up Mitcham Road. I went back inside, crying my eyes out. Lisa was still sitting in the lounge chair. She was shaking her head, saying, 'You poor thing. I know how dreadful this must be for you.' I asked her, 'What are we supposed to do? How can we stop her from doing this?' She shook her head and said, 'You can't. All you can do is be there for her.'

Kiersten, Alex and Josh were getting a bit sick of it. Alex wanted to leave home—he couldn't take all the tears and drama. I didn't blame him. I was on the verge of leaving myself. I had to front up for work every day and pretend that none of this was happening.

Othmar was struggling, too. My friends were trying to make me happy, to make me forget our problems. I didn't want to forget, I just wanted to be able to change it. Lisa left and wished me luck, saying, 'Ring me when Kartya comes back.' Kartya didn't come back. After twenty-four hours I went and reported her to the police as missing.

Joshua came home from school and told me that he had sighted Kartya at the drop-in centre. It was a place run by our local church where kids could meet after school, supposedly to keep them off the streets. It was run by a youth worker called Peter Nixon. I liked Peter. He worked with kids and really cared for them and understood them. Even though Kartya hadn't been going to school, she would meet up with her friends at the centre.

I hopped in my car and raced up there. When Kartya saw me, she started to run off. I called out, 'Kartya, I want to give you some money'. I knew she would come to me if I said that. She walked up, with her head hanging down. I asked her where she was staying and she said, 'Rebecca's.' I said, 'Who is Rebecca?' She replied, 'A friend.'

I asked her to come home. She said no. I asked her to come home for dinner. She said no. I asked her to come home and have a shower. She said no. She looked dirty, her beautiful long black hair needed a wash, her big baggy pants, all frayed on the bottom, needed a wash. I told her to look after herself and that if she wanted to come home, she could. Her lovely skin was all blotchy and her eyes were red. She looked tired and very unhappy.

I left her there, gave her my packet of cigarettes and twenty dollars, got in my car and drove back home. What choice did I have? If I could have dragged her home, I would have. Josh asked me how she was. I said, 'She looks tired. She looks like she hasn't slept and her eyes are all red.' He said to me, 'Mum, her eyes are red because she's probably smoking dope.'

I didn't know what he meant. I said, 'What sort of dope?'

'Marijuana, Mum,' said Josh. I realised that I didn't know anything about drugs. I didn't even know what dope was. How stupid could I be? I had thought the worst thing was that she had left home. Now I found out she was smoking marijuana. Straight away, I got on the phone and rang Peter Nixon at the drop-in centre. I asked him if it was possible that she could be smoking dope. He said, yes, she probably was. I asked him what I could do. I felt she was at risk. He said we should make a notification to Human Services to get Child Protection involved. I asked him if he would do that. I couldn't because I was a parent. He agreed.

I was angry with myself for giving her the twenty dollars. I thought, she's just going to go and buy some more of this dope stuff with it.

The next day the Human Services Child Protection Unit contacted us. Othmar and I impressed on the protection workers that we needed help. We could not control Kartya's behaviour and were unable to guarantee her safety. They suggested we go to court and obtain an Interim Protection Order. The judge made the order for three months on the grounds that Kartya was involved in marijuana use and her emotional and physical presentation and level of communication indicated that she was unable to adequately care for herself. Also that she had left home approximately one week prior to the notification being made and, during that time, had lived at a number of addresses, none of which she was willing to disclose. She was not willing to return home and had no plans for suitable safe accommodation. She was thirteen years old.

It was of some comfort to me and Othmar that we now had

some support. We needed it, we couldn't do it on our own. We now had someone to help us and somewhere to go. When Kartya heard that she had been placed on an Interim Protection Order, she was very angry. She said I should mind my own business and stay out of her life.

I told her, 'Kartya, your life is our life and your business is our business, regardless of what you think.' She was given the choice of coming home or going into a youth refuge. She decided to come home. We were all happy to have her back. Othmar and I told her that the same rules applied: she had to go to school and, if she wanted to go out, we would drive her and pick her up. She reluctantly agreed. It was while we were having dinner, discussing how we were going to work things out, that she said, 'Mum, I'm not going into one of those refuge places. All those kids are stuffed in the head, I'm not going to finish up like that.' She looked at me and I said, 'No, Kartya, you're definitely not going to finish up like that, not ever.' I put my arms around her and she tensed up. She still didn't want to be cuddled.

One day Othmar and I went to a Sunday market, just to walk around and get away by ourselves. We always enjoyed wandering around together, pretending that we had a normal life. The first place that I always headed for was the pet shop. I have always loved animals. Before we had kids, we had two poodles called Bimbo and Bambi. They were our babies. When Othmar and I went on holidays once, we put them both in boarding kennels. Bambi fretted so much we had to come home. They would sleep on our bed and I would cook them fillet steak for dinner.

I looked at all the little dogs in the cages and there was one sitting all alone. I opened the cage and took him out. He was a little Jack Russell pup, so small I could hold him in the palm of my hand. I said to Othmar, 'I want to buy him.' His eyes rolled into the back of his head as he said, 'What do you want a dog for. Haven't we got enough to look after?' I said, 'I want him for Kartya. If she can't love us, maybe she can love this little fellow.' He agreed with me. Little Jake became our new family member. I thought it might stop Kartya from going on her walkabouts if she had someone else to be responsible for.

When Kartya saw Jake she went nuts, she fell in love with him.

Jake was her dog. He would sleep in her bed, she would feed him and take him for walks. It was a positive distraction for her. It did keep her home for a while, but inevitably she lost interest in Jake. She started wandering again and left us to look after little Jake. Whenever she came back home he would go crazy, jumping all over her, but he was a bit scared of her. He didn't like it if she raised her voice. If she was in one of her moods and would start screaming and yelling, poor Jake would hide under the chair and no amount of coaxing would bring him out.

CHAPTER THIRTEEN
Chroming, Reiki and Court Appearances

When Kartya reluctantly put on her school uniform and went back to school, we breathed a sigh of relief. We felt that we had been mildly successful in containing her behaviour and keeping her within the limits of the family home. As she headed off, Othmar gave her a hug, wished her luck and made a cross on her forehead. He always did that with the kids, it was his way of imparting his religious beliefs to them. I prayed in my mind that the Lord would protect her and keep her at school.

Kartya didn't communicate with us much at home. She kept to herself. Whenever I would try and engage her in conversation, she would answer with monosyllables. Just a yes or a no. She went out with her friends and I would drive her and pick her up. I took her shopping to buy some new clothes. She didn't have many left because she would lend her clothes to 'friends' and never get them back. I bought her a new creamy white pair of jeans and some sneakers.

We thought that she was still smoking the dope stuff. Sometimes her eyes were red. I didn't confront her because I didn't want to face it. I was just happy she was going to school. Othmar and I talked about it and his thoughts were the same as mine: she could be taking worse, so let's leave it alone. I don't think either of us wanted to know. We couldn't think of anything else she could be taking anyway. She seemed fine, so we just left it.

Weeks later, she was complaining about a sore throat and she had a runny nose. Her cheeks always seemed to be bright red and she had become very aggressive again. She was reclusive, spending all her time in her bedroom. One night Alex, Kiersten, Joshua and I were watching television. Othmar was at work. Kartya was in her bedroom as usual.

We turned the television off to go to bed. I went to Kartya's room and knocked on her door to say goodnight. I always said goodnight to the kids. She screamed, 'Don't come in, Mum.' I pushed the door open and I said, 'Why not?' I could smell what I thought was nail polish remover. I asked her what she was doing. She screamed at me, 'Nothing, Mum. Just get out, just fucking get out.' Her face was all red, her lips were grey. She started pushing me out of the room. I saw a white plastic bag and a spray paint can on the floor. It still didn't dawn on me what she was doing. She was swaying around, unable to stand properly. I screamed to Alex, he came running upstairs. He said, 'Oh, my God, Mum, she's sniffing paint.'

I was crying, saying 'Kartya, why? Why are you doing this?' She was sobbing uncontrollably, saying, 'Mum, I don't know. I'm fucked in the head. Please help me, Mum, please help me.' I was shaking as I put my arms around her and told her that we would help her, that everything would be all right.

Alex was standing there in tears. He said, 'Kartya, if anything ever happens to you, none of us will ever be able to leave this house. Please don't do this, don't ever do it again.'

Kiersten and Josh were standing at the door with looks of bewilderment on their faces. I thought to myself that this was just not fair. Why do we all have to go through this pain? I cleaned up the paint and took away the bag, still in a daze. I'd never heard of anyone doing this: sniffing paint to get high. Then it occurred to me that she must have been doing it for weeks and we didn't even know. The red face, the runny nose, the sore throat. The new pair of jeans that I had been soaking in bleach, sometimes overnight, to get the little grey specks off. I thought it was grease from my washing machine. Here I am trying to get her pants clean, thinking it's grease, and all the while it's chrome paint.

The stuff splattered on her new sneakers that I saw her cleaning with mineral turps, that was paint too. How stupid could we be? How could we not have seen the signs? We thought we had big problems with her running away from home and smoking this dope stuff. How were we going to deal with this?

I got Kartya into bed and I lay beside her. I told her that no matter what happened we all loved her. We would always love her and we would always help her. I waited for Othmar to come home that night. I told him what had happened and he was shocked. He looked at me and said, 'What next?'

Next day I rang Child Protection and told them what happened the night before. The Protective Worker said, 'Oh, now she's involved in VSA.' I naively said, 'What's that?' She explained that it was Volatile Substance Abuse. Apparently it was quite common amongst young people; it was a cheap way of getting high. They would spray the chrome paint into a plastic bag and inhale the fumes. It could be fatal. Othmar and I both talked to Kartya. She knew the dangers and she promised us that she would never do it again.

I became paranoid. I would check in her room for paint tins or plastic bags. I would check her clothes for paint spots and question her whenever she had a runny nose. Once when I was giving her the third degree, asking her all sorts of questions as to where she'd been and what she was doing, she looked at me and said, 'Who do you think you are, Mum? You're not the fucking police. I don't have to tell you everything.' I said, 'Kartya, I am your mother and an unreal one at that.' She looked at me as if I was stupid. I thought to myself at that time, 'Kartya, if you would just give me half a chance to be your mother, then maybe we could sort this mess out. I'm doing the best I can. You didn't come with a book of instructions, all you came with was adoption papers that said you were the daughter of Lin-Ah-Hua. Maybe if we could find her, then all the pain and anger would go away.'

We never found any evidence that Kartya continued chroming. She told us she didn't and we believed her.

I contacted the Human Services Intercountry Adoption Department and asked them if they could help us find Kartya's birth family. They said they would try but told us that it could take quite a while.

Kartya needed to find some peace of mind. Her genetic links to her Chinese background were very strong; she didn't understand it and we didn't know how to help her. Her whole presence was so Chinese. She started buying her own food; she didn't like what we ate. She would buy dried beef that looked like the sole of an old shoe. She would squat on the floor eating it as if it was a lolly. Her Chinese vegetables and noodles filled the refrigerator, leaving no room for anything else. She would smother her Chinese sausages in a combination of soy sauce, fish sauce and chilli sauce. Her taste buds were certainly different from ours. People would ask us why, when she'd lived all her life with us, she liked everything Chinese. We didn't know. We just knew that it was in her, it had been from the very beginning. The blood running through her veins was Chinese and nothing and no-one was going to be able to change that. That is why she felt different. She felt like she didn't fit in anywhere. Othmar and I understood that, we could see that she was struggling with her identity and that was why we had to help her through her problems. They were all symptoms of her internal fight to feel at peace with herself.

I can't understand why someone hasn't invented a little pill that you could give teenagers when they got revolting and out of control. You could give it to them and they would be nice and well-mannered and not destroy your self-esteem. Someone told me about an eastern form of healing called reiki. I decided to investigate, thinking that it might help to heal Kartya. We were prepared to try anything, even though we weren't all that sure exactly what the problem was. We found that reiki means universal life energy. Not that Kartya needed extra energy, she had plenty of that, it was just that it was all channelled in the wrong direction. The practice of reiki instils inner harmony. It is an ancient healing method where the practitioner uses their hands to direct positive energy to the patient to create emotional and mental healing and give a feeling of wellbeing . . . seeing Kartya was full of unwellbeing, I thought that a dose of wellbeing wouldn't go astray. Reiki can also help cure depression and feelings of helplessness. It helps to balance the energies in your body, making you more able to cope with the problems from within. It gives you a calmer approach to dealing with problems that have become insurmountable. I couldn't help but feel that maybe I was the one who should be getting reikied. I had to just stand at the back of the queue, with all the other mothers.

Reiki can help to release past suppressed feelings, especially feelings of anger and sadness. It can create an inner expression of love for yourself and give you courage to change things in your life. If you are open to receiving reiki it can balance your whole mind, body and soul. Othmar and I decided to take Kartya along, to give it a try. The family finances didn't exactly stretch to the thirty dollars needed for each half-hour session, but we thought that if it worked, it would be good value for money.

We booked in and took Kartya along to a private home in Glen Iris. The reiki practitioner was a very strange-looking lady, with long flowing red hair and a bright pink kaftan. The red and pink didn't exactly match, but I didn't hold that against her as she was highly recommended by our local doctor. Kartya was very enthusiastic about trying it. After the first session, she came out as if she was in a trance. She was very subdued and, on the way home in the car, she talked to me. I felt that alone was worth thirty dollars. She said to me, 'Mum, it made me feel really peaceful.' When we got home, I quickly rang the red-haired lady in the pink kaftan and booked another session. We'd probably be eating baked beans for the next week, but I thought the thirty dollars was worth it if it made her feel peaceful. We continued going twice a week for about five weeks. I would race home from work, pick up Kartya and drive all the way across town to the reiki lady. Kartya would go in for her session and I would collapse in the chair in her waiting room, exhausted.

The positive thing was that it did seem to be helping Kartya. She was sleeping better at night and even though she was still very hot-headed she seemed to be putting the brakes on her anger.

When she talked to me, she communicated in sentences and not just monosyllables. She would say to me, 'Mum, I love going to reiki. Can I go as long as I like?' My answer was, 'As long as I can find sixty dollars a week for the two sessions, and the other kids don't mind sausages and baked beans, then you can go.' I honestly don't know what I thought the long-term outcome of the sessions would be. I think I hoped that it would keep her in a calmer frame of mind, at least until we could find Lin-Ah-Hua. I was hoping that it would take away her need to use the dope stuff in order to make her feel calm. I would buy cigarettes for her, only because if I didn't she would pinch mine and I would be left with none. After all, I needed to have something to help me through the day, and sometimes a cigarette was the only crutch I had. I enjoyed my few glasses of wine, but I needed to restrict myself, just in case I got a phone call at a ridiculous hour to go and pick up a daughter who had gone walkabout.

Our helter-skelter life continued unabated, with me having mini nervous breakdowns every time I forgot to put on my hormone patch. I had enough to think about without trying to remember that. After all, I was racing off to reiki twice a week, working full time and trying to keep all the bits of our life together. I was driving an old car that spewed exhaust fumes into the cabin, so I would drive with a handkerchief tied around my face so as not to inhale the fumes. Maybe a few gulps would have made me feel a bit calmer, but one in the family with an addictive personality was enough, I was walking around in a trance often enough as it was.

When I heard Kartya upstairs in her bedroom, kicking in the walls again, I decided that the running around after reiki had reached its ending. I began to think that it hadn't made a difference; it had all been in my mind. She was still very angry, very sad and unable to control her emotions. I wanted to ring up the lady with the long red hair and the pink kaftan and ask for a refund. Instead I decided to use the money on myself. I booked myself into a masseur named Reg who was legally blind. For twenty-five dollars I had a weekly massage. I had gone from the end of the queue to the top. I was now going to look after myself first, every week.

Kartya continued going to school even though she was constantly getting into trouble. She would get suspended every second week. She didn't care; it gave her an excuse not to go to school. She got into trouble for smoking at school and leaving her butts on the sports oval. She was accused of setting fire to a rubbish bin, even though she said she didn't do it. One day I was called to the school because they said she had been drinking alcohol in the school toilets. When I picked her up, she reeked of alcohol, although she didn't appear to have been drinking it. She told me that some girls had brought a bottle to school and poured it over the top of her. I believed her. She felt that she got the blame because she was already in trouble over the smoking issue. She was given a two-week detention.

Her inability to cope with her anger was one of the main issues that concerned the school, and her refusal to go to counselling didn't help. She continued to be abusive and to use unacceptable language at school, and at home things were not much better. We continued to fight over discipline issues. She would walk in and out of home as if it were a five-star hotel. On one occasion when she just upped and left, she rang me from the local fun-parlour and said, 'Mum, I left my smokes behind. Can you bring them up?' She would make me so angry. She had such cheek. It was as if she had no conscience whatsoever. It almost made you think that her behaviour was normal. When I refused to take her cigarettes to her, she rang and told me that I was a selfish bitch. I would take refuge in my favourite chair, covered in Sanderson linen, with big cabbage roses over it, and shake my head.

Kartya went back to school in Year 8, but that didn't last long. She refused to accept authority, continued to abuse the teachers and kept walking out of class. When she had an altercation with one teacher and walked out of class down the corridor yelling 'Fuck all teachers' they expelled her. They didn't want her back. She was free at last, that's what she wanted. She didn't want to be tied down. She wanted to control her own life and nothing and nobody was going to interfere with that. I tried to get her enrolled in other schools in the area, but they didn't want her either. The fact was that I was trying to organise her life. She simply didn't want that. She had decided that it was much more fun roaming the streets with her friends. Othmar and I hoped that in time she would get bored, wake up to herself and go back to school.

Not being at school meant that Kartya was getting into trouble on the streets. She got caught for stealing a pair of boxer shorts at a department store. The shop security lady caught her and Kartya kicked her in the shins. I told Kartya that if she had been at school where she belonged then it would never have happened. We had to go to court as she was charged with shoplifting and assault. When we met her solicitor outside the court, he looked at me and said, 'And who may you be?' Before I could answer, Kartya said, 'My mother. Who do you think?' I laughed to myself. One minute she didn't want me as her mother and the next she expected people to recognise me as her mother. On the outside we didn't look anything like mother and daughter.

I found it very strange that Kartya seemed to know half the other kids at court. She would go outside and have a smoke with them. They all knew each other. They were quite a little family, these kids who didn't go to school and walked around the streets getting into trouble.

We became frustrated with Kartya because she would always say to me, 'That's it, Mum. I'm not going to finish up here ever again.' Lo and behold, a month or so later we would be back in court again for another misdemeanour. I contemplated taking up knitting so I could do something productive on my days spent in court. I figured that I would probably be able to knit everyone in the family a jumper in the amount of time I spent there. But I decided against that idea because my children were all past wearing handknitted things. They were only interested in living in a normal family again. Somehow I felt that we all still had a long road ahead of us.

CHAPTER FOURTEEN

Breakdown

$\mathscr{I}$ got one of those phones with a key in it. I was sick of getting hundreds of dollars of phone bills that I couldn't pay. All of Kartya's friends seemed to have mobile phones and she'd be on the phone to them for hours on end. Every time anyone in the family wanted to make a phone call they had to ask me for the key. It worked fine for a while—until I lost the key. I gave up in the end. I consoled myself with the fact that if Kartya was at home in her room on the phone, then at least she wasn't roaming around the streets.

I was in the habit of cooking our evening meal one night ahead, so that every night I would just have to heat up the meal when I got home. This particular night, I had a big tray of lasagne in the oven.

Kartya's antics were exhausting me. I was always tired and stressed out. It was like living on a merry-go-round. It just kept going around and around and I couldn't get off. Sometimes it would be going in slow motion and other times at hundreds of miles an hour. I always seemed to have a headache.

I dragged my weary body—what was left of it, I was like a stick, I had lost so much weight—upstairs to get ready for bed. Kartya was in her room on the phone. She'd been on it for hours. I called out, 'Kartya, get off the phone. I'm going to bed.' She didn't answer me. I went into the bathroom and brushed my teeth. I went back and she was still on the phone. I knocked on her door and opened it. I said, 'Kartya, get off that bloody phone now.'

She started screaming and yelling abuse at me, then picked up the phone and threw it at me. I started to feel dizzy, my heart was racing and my head was hurting. My chest felt tight. Then my legs just gave away from under me. I fell to the floor. I was having trouble breathing. Josh came in and I heard him scream at Kartya, 'Quick, call an ambulance.'

I heard Kartya vaguely in the background, saying, 'My mum's fainted. She can't breathe, come quickly.'

Josh and Kiersten knelt beside me. Josh was saying, 'Mum, breathe. Please, Mum, just keep breathing.' My breathing was very shallow; I couldn't get my breath. Next thing I knew the lady from next door was kneeling beside me, holding my hand saying, 'Don't worry, the ambulance will be here soon.'

The ambulance arrived and they loaded me onto a stretcher and put me in the back. Off they took me to hospital with the siren blaring. I lay there in the back, feeling very disoriented when I suddenly thought, 'God, I left the lasagne in the oven.'

The kids rang Othmar at work. He came straight home, picked up the kids and came to hospital. The first thing I said to him, was 'Did the lasagne burn?' He held my hand and said, 'I think the last thing you should be worrying about is the lasagne.'

I couldn't remember much of what had happened. My mind was a blank. Kartya was standing at the end of the bed. Her chin was jutting out, her lips were pursed, and she had an angry look on her face. I held out my hand to her, but she just stood there. She wouldn't come near me. Othmar shook his head at me, as if to say, 'Just leave her.' It wasn't until later that he told me she blamed herself; she thought it was all her fault. I tried to explain to Kartya that we didn't blame her; that it happened because I was tired and run down. Not because she threw the phone at me. The hospital released me the next day and told me that my breakdown was a warning sign. They said I should slow down and take things easy and try not to get myself into stressful situations. How I was going to achieve that, I had no idea.

The thought occurred to me that I could just leave home. After all, if Kartya could do it, then why couldn't I? Maybe I could go back and live with Mum and Dad. I'm sure they would have loved to have had me. I could sleep in the bungalow, with the earwigs. The little black things with the long tentacles. At least they would be less offensive than an uncontrollable adolescent. Mum would bring me breakfast in bed: Vegemite on toast and a cup of tea. The thought was an attractive option, but not very realistic. I thought of what my mum would have done. She wouldn't have given up. She would never have walked away from any of her kids; neither would my dad. She always said that we were perfect. We weren't; it was just the way she saw us, all ten of us. When I thought of her, it inspired me to go on. My mother, the perfect mother. Why did she have to be so damn good? Maybe then I wouldn't have striven to be so much like her. It was as if someone up there was saying to me and Othmar: You think you're so damn smart. Take this child and see how smart you really are.

I would say to myself: We haven't come this far to give up on you now, Kartya. If you think we will, then you've got another think coming.

The decisions that we had to make involved the whole family, not just for the moment, but for the future. We had to consider how the other kids would see the decisions we made today, in two or five years time. Were they going to thank us if we gave up on Kartya, the sister they loved, or were they going to thank us for hanging in there and believing that we all still had a future together? None of us liked what was happening in our family; it put enormous pressure on everyone. We didn't have a normal life. Every minute of it was taken up with Kartya. The whole family's lives revolved around what was happening with Kartya.

When I first met Chris Bull, I fell in love with him immediately. With his big build and his bushy beard, he looked like Father Christmas. It was his eyes that told me he cared about kids. They were compassionate and caring. Our family had been referred to Wesley Youth Services for support to help Kartya with her problems. She was on a good behaviour bond and was slowly climbing up the Juvenile Justice System ladder. Kartya related to Chris from the very beginning. I think she felt he treated her like a person and not a delinquent. She could communicate with him better than with anyone else. He would jokingly call her a little ratbag. He knew that our family needed help, that we wanted to help Kartya and we were not giving up. He supported us and Kartya as much as he could.

She had gone walkabout and didn't tell us where so we reported her missing to the police. She was plucked off the streets and ordered by the court to live in a Wesley Youth Refuge. It was a normal suburban house, only a five-minute drive from our house in Mitcham Road. Kartya liked being there, I think, because it was close to us. Even though she would carry on and continue to abuse us, we never really believed she meant it, because she always wanted to have contact with us, especially with me. She would ring me and say, 'Mum, who's home? What are you doing? What are you having for dinner?' If it was something she liked, she would ask me to come and get her, and she would come home for dinner.

Kartya felt quite at home at the refuge. They did help her and she responded to the guidelines and discipline most of the time. Chris was always there to support the kids, and he was a great support to me and Othmar. I was always ringing him for advice. Sometimes twice a day. He didn't mind. He knew how we felt.

Kartya was still wanting to find Lin-Ah-Hua, her birth mother, and we had written lots of letters trying to find her. They all came back negative. We received a letter from the Human Services Intercountry Adoption Department stating that Lin-Ah-Hua had moved addresses and they were unable to find a forwarding place of residence. Kartya would get quite despondent and say, 'Why doesn't my mother try and find me?' I would explain to her that maybe her mother didn't know that she had come to Australia. Kartya would say, 'Mum, she can't be looking too fucking hard. It's not like I'd be that hard to find.' She would make me laugh. I loved her so much. Life to her was so simple: if you want to do something, you just go and do it. It made us think that this birth mother of hers must be some lady. Kartya didn't get her tough crusty exterior from nowhere. It was in her for a reason, it came from somewhere. I just wished we knew where. The whole family was getting dragged on this journey to God knows where and we all wanted to know why. I would think to myself: Do we get a reward at the end, or a punishment?

Kartya stayed at the refuge for almost a year. She spent her fourteenth birthday there. She was having counselling from a psychologist at the Human Services Juvenile Justice Unit, a wonderful lady called Ros Harris. I had the greatest respect for Ros, because she understood Kartya. She could see the pain that Kartya was experiencing and tried very hard to help her talk through her problems. She had no doubt that Kartya was suffering from Reactive Attachment Disorder, and a lot of her anger was from issues relating to her early abandonment. It was for this reason that we felt that Kartya had great difficulty in accepting boundaries and trusting others. She had no inner belief that anyone really cared for her.

Kartya realised that she struggled daily with her inability to control herself. Sometimes she would say to me, 'Mum, I don't even know why I do the stupid things I do.' I didn't have an answer for her, either. I could only try to encourage her to talk to Ros and try to work through the reasons for her anger. When I felt like throwing in the towel, I would ring Ros. She would give me the strength inside to continue on the journey.

I always liked people who saw the good in our daughter. People who took the time to get to know her saw the vulnerable side, her wonderful sense of humour, her commitment to us, albeit shown in an unusual way. People who didn't take the time didn't see that side to her. They only saw the rebellious little bitch. I didn't like them. It had to be that way, otherwise it was too hard. I wasn't open to negative conversations about Kartya. We, of all people, her family, knew her shortcomings, we didn't need to be told. The only way we could help Kartya was to focus on the positive steps she was making, even though most times she walked backwards instead of forwards.

Walking away from her was simply never an option. If Kartya had a huge growth growing on the outside of her heart, where everyone could see it, people would expect us to help her. Because the huge growth was growing inside her heart, where nobody could see it, didn't mean that we shouldn't stick by her and help her get rid of it.

Kartya outgrew the refuge. She left and started to wander again. Her walkabouts took her far afield. Whatever she was looking for she did a good job of trying to find it because she would pop up in all sorts of suburbs around Melbourne. She discovered Springvale and she loved it. She once told me, 'Mum, I've never seen so many Asians in the one place all at the same time.' Most of her friends were Asian boys; not boyfriends, just friends. They looked on her as a little sister. She would call them her brothers.

I suppose she felt like one of them: she looked like them, liked the same food. She didn't feel like the odd one out. A friend of mine once said to me, 'Nola, I wouldn't be too happy about Kartya spending all her time with those Asian boys, they all use and sell heroin.' I said, 'No, I don't think so. Anyway, Kartya wouldn't use that stuff—she hates needles.' Othmar and I would talk about the drug thing; we didn't think she was using anything. She would come home from time to time, usually after she had rung me and I'd told her that I'd reported her as a missing person. She'd be fine for a couple of days, then we'd have a huge fight, and off she'd go again. I'd go and report her missing again after twenty-four hours. We reported her as a missing person sixteen times in all. She hated it when she knew I'd reported her missing. She once said to me, 'Mum, if the cops find me, it'll be all your fault.' I thought, Well, that's the whole idea, Kartya. With a bit of luck, one day they will find you and make you come back home. At times I felt like dragging her home by the scruff of the neck and giving her a good hiding with the wooden spoon. I knew I wouldn't and I knew I couldn't.

The whole family was feeling battle-worn. I was tired all the time. I couldn't sleep. It's hard to sleep when you don't know where your child is, when you don't know if they're alive or dead. Othmar was carrying his pain inside, I could tell by his face. Kiersten, Alex and Josh didn't communicate all that much with Kartya when she came and went. I understood because they had trouble understanding why she was leading the life she was, and in the process of that, making all of us miserable. They didn't like it when she came home and all the screaming and yelling started again. They did care about her, but they knew that nobody could stop her from doing what she wanted to.

There were times when I thought that my sanity was severely impaired. I always seemed to be yelling at everyone. I was arguing with Othmar and being unreasonable with the other kids. I was feeling guilty for spending every minute of every day trying to solve Kartya's problems. Whenever she would ring me, I would drop everything and go to her aid. I apologised to the other kids, because I felt like I was neglecting their needs. Kiersten put her arms around me and said, 'Mum, don't worry we understand. Kartya needs you more at the moment, we're fine.' I knew they understood, but I still felt guilty.

One day I went to a big shopping centre to do some shopping and parked my car in the car park. I went into the supermarket and did all my food shopping, came out and couldn't remember where I'd parked my car. I wandered around the car park in a daze with my full trolley load of shopping, unable to even remember what colour my car was. I sat down and cried my eyes out, like a big baby. A lovely lady came with me to try and find the registration number of my car that was on my key ring. When we found my car, she helped me put my shopping in the boot, then put her arm on my shoulder and said, 'Don't worry, dear. It happens to me all the time.' The fact that she was about twenty years older than me didn't make me feel much better. I thought, That's it, I am definitely going crazy. If all this doesn't stop soon, I'm going to finish up in the nut house.

Some days I would drag myself wearily upstairs into our bedroom, sit up in my big brass bed and look out of the big windows. I could see the mountains from up there. It was peaceful and tranquil. I often did this when I was stressed. I loved that room, it was my little oasis.

I was always a bit reluctant to ring my mum in Geelong and tell her what was happening with Kartya, because we would both get upset. So I would avoid ringing her.

I had let weeks go by. Finally I sat on my bed, picked up the phone and rang her. I made myself a promise that I wouldn't get upset. The first thing she said was, 'Nola, what's happening with Kartya?' I just burst into tears and said, 'Mum, I don't even know where she is.' Mum was crying. She tried to tell me that it would all work out. She tried to be reassuring. This wonderful mother of ten, grandmother of thirty-two. I asked her, 'Mum, what would you do if you were me?' She said, 'Well, Nola, I wouldn't give up, if that's what you mean. I would never have given up on any of you kids.' I thought, Thanks Mum, that's all I needed to hear.

It strengthened my resolve to keep going, to keep putting one foot in front of the other without tripping over and falling flat on my face. Thanks, Mum, the mum who at twenty-one I couldn't wait to get away from because I didn't want to finish up like her. Here I was becoming more like her every day. She had been my teacher when I wasn't even aware that I was her student. My lovely Mum and Dad who treated our two adopted girls as their own. Kiersten worshipped her nanna. She would write her letters and Nanna would write back to her. Kartya was more partial to

Pop. She would always stand beside his chair in the hope that he would give her some money or sweets. It would be unusual for Pop if Kartya didn't stand beside his chair. He would think that there was something wrong with her. He did tell me once that Kartya's behaviour left a lot to be desired. I said to him, 'I know, Dad, but I'm doing the best that I can. It's just that she won't listen to anyone.' He looked up, and said, 'Yes, Nola, I've noticed.'

Away

Take me away from this mad world of mine
I don't want to be here, is that a crime?
I can't cope with this any more
For years it's gone on, what for?
I tried my best to fix all the pain
I don't have the strength to try again
If I go away, I won't come back
I go to my room and start to pack
I throw everything into this bag of mine
Go to the fridge, grab a bottle of wine
I'll make my escape, while no-one's here
turn my back on them all
and make one thing clear
I'm not coming back to this mad world of mine
I'll go somewhere quiet and knock off my wine
In the end, I'll be the one who comes out the winner
Just as I leave to walk out the door
Josh comes home and says, 'Mum, what's for dinner?'
I don't have the heart to leave them alone
I go to my room and unpack my bag
Wipe away my tears with a torn bit of rag
Open my wine and pour a glass
tell myself that it was all just a farce
Me, walking away from this mad world of mine.

CHAPTER FIFTEEN
Out of Control

⁓⁓

*A*fter I had my little wobbly—fell flat on the floor and got carted off to hospital in the ambulance—I thought that I needed a bit of help to handle the daily dramas that unfolded constantly. Someone told me about a parent support group that met once a week to help and encourage parents to get through a crisis. I talked to Othmar about it and he thought it would be a good idea. He couldn't come, as he was working at night, but felt I should give it a go. I certainly needed help. I felt like I was walking around and around in circles, getting nowhere.

I took myself along one Wednesday night to this big hall at the local church. There must have been about fifty people there. I thought, Surely not all these people have problems with their kids. We were split up into five groups of about ten people by this big bossy lady who ran the meeting. She told us that her son was addicted to heroin. He had become a junkie and had stolen from them and broken all the windows in the family home. I wanted to ask her when a person addicted to heroin crosses the line and becomes a junkie. It sounded like she was talking about two different people. She told us that she had not had any contact with her son for two years and that the whole episode had broken up her marriage. I must say that I didn't feel all that confident about taking any advice from her.

I was placed in a group with two men and two other women. We all introduced ourselves. One big burly gentleman introduced himself as a police sergeant, the other man was an accountant. One of the ladies was a primary school teacher and the other a computer operator. They looked at me strangely when I introduced myself as a mother. The group practised the 'tough love' method of discipline. You lay down the guidelines and if the child doesn't abide by the rules, you kick them out. I felt uncomfortable with that, to say the least. I thought, If your kid has problems, and you turn your back on them, where do they go? Who do they turn to? The computer operator lady told us that her son was sixteen, and he had burnt her house down. The primary school teacher's daughter was addicted to heroin, had left home at fourteen and had become a prostitute to support her habit. The accountant said that his son was a schizophrenic, due to the amount of marijuana he smoked, and the big burly policeman said that his son had stolen everything from their house, and sold it all to support a drug habit. He had charged him with burglary and theft and he was convicted and jailed. He had a smile on his face when he told us.

I felt very uncomfortable. I was feeling more depressed by the minute. Everyone was talking about how bad their kids were. No-one was talking about why their kids might have been doing these things. I went away from the meeting thinking that my problems were not all that bad—a daughter who smokes the dope stuff and inhales paint fumes. I'm not going back there again, I thought. I'll just go home and Othmar and I will handle it all. Our daughter is not as bad as that. I'll just continue to be my daughter's unreal mother. Surely, in the end, that will count for something. I'll just continue to try and be optimistic and hope that a solution will be around the corner. I just wished I knew which corner to look around.

When I got home, Kiersten and Josh asked me how I went. I told them how I felt about the meeting and they said, 'Mum, you don't need to hear about everyone else's problems. We've got enough of our own.' Somehow I agreed with them.

Kartya continued wandering in and out of home. We weren't happy about it, but when she turned up, and she was breathing, I was relieved that at least she was all right. She would stay a few days and then leave. One day she was in her bedroom, talking on the phone to a friend. I don't know what she was on, but she was so happy, laughing hysterically, it was unusual to hear her so happy. I was tempted to knock on her door and ask her if I could have some of whatever she was taking; maybe it would make me laugh, too.

It was around this time she brought home a boy she wanted Othmar and me to meet. His name was Tran. He was Vietnamese. She introduced him to us as her boyfriend. He was very quiet and shy. He looked about nineteen years old. I can't say we didn't like him, he seemed pleasant enough. He appeared to care about Kartya, and she was all over him. Sitting on his knee and calling him honey. She seemed to be very happy with him. We thought that it was a positive sign that she seemed to have formed an attachment to someone. When she wasn't staying at home with us, she was at Tran's house with his mother and three sisters. I told myself that at least she was safe there. If she was with him, she was not on the streets. She would come and go, in and out of home. Sometimes at Tran's and sometimes with 'friends'. We never got to know their names.

I don't know when Othmar and I first realised that Kartya was using heroin. Deep down, I think we both suspected it, but we didn't want to face it. We thought it would just go away. Our suspicions were confirmed one day when Tran was charged by the police for offences relating to heroin. Kartya just came straight out and told us. 'Mum, you know I'm using heroin.' I said, 'Yes, I know you are, Kartya.' I knew she was. I didn't want to hear it. My heart sank. I knew then that we had big problems, very big problems. When I told Othmar, his face dropped. He just looked at me and said, 'What do we do now?' I didn't know, but I was sure of one thing: unless we solved the reasons why Kartya was so sad and depressed, nothing would change. Was the answer to find Lin-Ah-Hua, her birth mother? I was sure that was the need that was eating her up and spitting her out. You didn't need to have a degree in psychology to figure that out. Blind Freddie could see it. Our thoughts were confirmed when Kartya left extracts from her diary on her bedroom floor. When we read the pages we panicked. Then we knew how much her life was out of control.

Dear Diary, All I want to do is die, so that everything will be gone. No-one knows this pain I feel. No-one understands what I am going through. No-one understands why I choose to take drugs. It's the pain in my heart that no-one can see, it's the pain in my heart that leads me to choose this life. It's not a life I want, but I've gone too far to turn back and start again. No-one will ever understand the pain I'm going through. That is why I choose this life right now, because it takes away everything that I am feeling. All this hurt just disappears when I take this drug, it all just goes away. It's a heaven that you don't want to escape from. But this pain that I'm feeling, wanting to know who I am, is killing me. Yes, I can see it, but I don't give a shit. If I can't find the answers, then I might as well take the easy way out. I can't and I don't want to feel the pain that I am constantly feeling, it is just driving me crazy. Oh, God, is there someone out there that will help me?

It's been four months since I started using heroin heavily. It's my need to know where I came from, who are my parents, why did they give me away, and the most important question. WHO AM I?

This frustration and pain inside my mind and my heart is driving me crazy, so I take the needle and put it in my arm, to take the pain away. I want to know who I am so badly. I'll just keep on using it until I eventually fade away, then I won't hurt any more, then my pain will be taken away completely. Please help me find the answers to these questions that I've longed for so much. It's killing me, mentally and physically. The only way I can express my thoughts and feelings is on paper, to you, My Diary, and through poems.

Want to be Free

The shadow that follows me
haunts me for years.
The feeling of being free
will come only in tears.
I walk, feeling high
I've been wishing for years
of just saying goodbye.
This world being on drugs
has captured my life
and there's no turning back.
I wish I could end
my sad painful life.
Just one more won't hurt,
Please, just one more hit . . .

Words on paper are always worse than the spoken word. To read the words over and over about the deep pain that Kartya was feeling made Othmar and me feel totally helpless. She was on a journey and no-one could know where she was going to end up. I wanted to be able to put my arms around her and take all the pain away, but the love that we had for her was not enough. She needed answers to questions. Answers that we couldn't give her. I made a mental note that the next day I would go to the place in the city where they have phone books from all over the world and I would get the Taiwan phone book and photocopy some addresses and send some more letters to Taipei and try once again to track down Lin-Ah-Hua.

We felt desperate. We not only had the knowledge of Kartya's heroin addiction, but also the fact that she was contemplating suicide. We had reached a stage where the only important thing to all of us was to keep her alive.

The pressure on the whole family was taking its toll. It wasn't easy for me, always being home on my own when another drama unfolded. Just me and the kids. Othmar was only home on Sunday and Monday nights. The other nights he was out working. He was hardly ever there when the shit hit the fan. I resented that sometimes, unreasonably so. I was becoming a very unreasonable unreal mother. I always seemed to be the bad guy. When Othmar was home, Kartya was all sweetness and light.

I had taken to doing some craft activities at home, particularly decoupage. It made me concentrate on something other than my sadness. One night I was sitting at the kitchen table having a few glasses of wine. My pictures were all spread out everywhere, surrounding the big glass ashtray that I would fill with sticky white glue which I would use to stick my pictures down onto my large sheet of white cardboard. Othmar was standing in front of the big slate fireplace. We were talking about Kartya, our normal topic of conversation. All the kids were in bed, except Kartya. We didn't know where she was. I said to Othmar, 'Maybe if you were here more often, you'd be able to help me keep her under control.' I knew when I said it that I was being unfair. He said, 'Your problem is, you overreact. She doesn't come home and you go hysterical.' I had probably had too many glasses of wine, but he had pressed the wrong button. I picked up the ashtray full of glue and hurled it at him. It missed Othmar and hit the slate fireplace and shattered into a million pieces. There was glass and glue splattered everywhere. Poor Othmar looked stunned. I picked up my drink and went upstairs. I cried myself to sleep. The next morning, I felt guilty. I apologised and told him I was glad that the ashtray had missed him. I said to him, 'I knew I shouldn't have had that last glass of wine.' He looked at me and said, 'Well, I wasn't wrong. You did overreact and go hysterical.' We hugged each other.

All this was putting a big strain on our relationship, this heavy load we had to carry. We were both aware of it, so we tried to support each other and retain some of our sense of humour. If we lost that, we were dead and buried. I was vacuuming up bits of glass out of the shag pile carpet and picking bits of glue off the walls and curtains for months.

When Kartya told us that Tran had been jailed for twelve months for the offences relating to heroin, we weren't that surprised. We were worried about Kartya, though, and what effect this would have on her frame of mind. We knew she would be depressed because she did love him. We were also worried because now she would be staying with her so-called friends. At least when she was at Tran's we knew where to reach her. We asked her to come back home to live. She said, 'Mum, I can't. I can't come back home. Not the way I am.' I said to her, 'Kartya, we know the way you are and we want you to come back home.' She wouldn't consider it. She wanted to be with her army of friends. We knew that it would only be a matter of time before the police caught up with her because we told her that if we didn't hear from her every twenty-four hours, we would report her as a missing person to the police.

Stay A While ... Please

Stay a while
don't go out again
in the black of night
to God knows where
Stay a while
so I can tuck you into bed
make you some homemade soup
feed you till you're healthy
Stay a while
so I can mend your broken heart
take away the pain
fill the big black hole inside
Stay a while
don't go out again
in the black of night
to God knows where
and put a needle in your arm
Stay a while ... please

CHAPTER SIXTEEN
Lost Daughter

One day when I was at the local supermarket doing my weekly shopping, I met a friend who had a daughter the same age as Kartya. Both girls had gone to primary school together. I had often been to her house for morning teas and school get-togethers. She had only one child. We were chatting about our kids when she said, 'Oh, by the way, I hear you're having some problems with Kartya.' I said to her, 'Yes, she has got some problems. We're really worried. She's using heroin.' My friend looked shocked. She said, 'Oh God, I wouldn't go telling everyone that.' I said, 'Why not?' She answered, 'If my child was on heroin, I wouldn't tell everyone. How embarrassing. Aren't you ashamed of her?' I said, 'No, as a matter of fact, I'm not. I'm not embarrassed and I'm not ashamed, and people like you give me the shits.' I was so angry. I turned and walked away, leaving her with her mouth open and my trolley full of groceries standing in the aisle. I never saw her again.

I couldn't bear it when people didn't understand. We didn't like what Kartya was doing, not one bit, but we did try to understand why. Kiersten, Alex and Josh stood by her. They didn't give up. They weren't ashamed of her. It was as if being addicted to heroin all of a sudden made you a bad person, a criminal, someone to toss away, throw on the scrap heap. Why did people feel so uncomfortable when we talked about it? It wasn't a contagious disease.

We could see the way people reacted when we mentioned it. It seemed as if all of a sudden, in their eyes, we had become bad parents. It was our fault. We had done something wrong. One of the ladies who used to babysit the kids met me on the street and while commiserating with me said, 'Nola, this whole thing must be so dreadful for you and Othmar—but just think how much worse you would feel if it happened to your own child.' I was a bit puzzled. I said, 'What do you mean?' She answered, 'Well, with Kartya being adopted and that, she's probably of bad blood.' I just looked at her. I couldn't believe my ears. I smiled at her and walked off, because if I didn't do that I would have knocked her head off her shoulders and, seeing she was about sixty years old, I thought it would have been unfair. I thought, you have no idea, lady, no idea at all. I was biting the inside of my lip until it bled. I thought, that's what's going to happen to me. I'll bleed to death before this journey's over.

We all decided to go out for Mother's Day. I booked a table at a local restaurant. Othmar had to work, but Kiersten, Alex and Josh wanted to treat me for my special day. They were always trying to make things happier for me. Kartya had rung two nights before and, as usual, I had invited her along. She asked me who was going to be there. When I told her, she said that she would think about it. I wasn't all that optimistic that she would turn up because she didn't like being confronted with the other kids. It wasn't that they made her feel uncomfortable, it was more a case of her feeling guilty about everything. I knew that she did want to be with us, but because of her illness she couldn't begin to overcome the barriers that had grown up between all of us. She didn't turn up for lunch, so we went and had a lovely time together, me and the other kids. When we got home, Kartya had been and left a letter in the box.

To Dear Mum, Well, I don't really know where to start, I have never really written you a proper letter before. I know that I'm not the greatest daughter you would have dreamed of me to be, I hope one day I can be.

Me coming with you today is out of the question, I know that, because whenever we are together, we always seem to fight.

I seem to think that it's all my fault, when you have those breakdowns, I cry, because I know that I have hurt the family. It hurts me to see what I make the family go through.

I don't like it when we fight, and I always wish for the time when I can stop being a rebellious little bitch and start to realise what is happening in my life. You may not think that I love you, but deep down inside, I do love you. It's not only you that's hurting; it's me as well.

I don't mean for the family to go through what I have done to you all. I am not asking you for forgiveness, I am asking you to love me and stick by me, please. The reason why I go to heroin is because it takes all my problems away, I don't know any other way, I am sorry. I am also sorry I didn't get you a Mother's Day present, but I hope you like the poem that I wrote for you.

We loved, We laughed, We cried
You watched over me
a Mother with pride
I didn't have to say
But, yes, you knew
I loved you through and through
'I MISS YOU'

your daughter, Kartya.

When I read her letter, I cried for my lost daughter who was unable to accept the love and help that we were all prepared to give. I could only hope that with our continued expressions of support, one day she would feel part of the family and strong enough to face the pain and turmoil of her life. But I did feel that it was going to be quite a long time before anything changed. I sat down and wrote her a poem.

We Care

What can we do to help your pain
whatever we do, seems to be in vain.
We toss and turn
can't sleep at night
We're just trying to do
what we think is right
We look for you here
and we look for you there
and when we find you
you say you don't care
But we don't believe you
when we see your face
It tells us, you'd rather be in some other place
somewhere safe and warm and loved
Please come home
we can start again. From the very beginning
and get it right, give us a chance
Please come home
and we can start again . . .

CHAPTER SEVENTEEN
Missing Person

Othmar and I were under the impression that if we reported Kartya as a missing person to the police they would, if they found her, bring her home. I had given them a photo of her. Then one night I got a call from the local police station to tell me they had found Kartya. I was so relieved. I called out to the kids, 'The police have found her.' I asked the constable if I could come and get her. He said, 'Oh, she's not here. We had to let her go. She said she didn't want to come home. As she hadn't committed any offence, we couldn't hold her. I'm just letting you know that we're taking her off the missing persons' list.' I was flabbergasted and angry. I couldn't believe it. What was the point in reporting her missing if they just let her go? I said to the constable, 'You know, our daughter is using heroin.' He answered, 'She seemed fine. She had no drugs on her person and we simply don't have the power to make a young person return home if they don't want to.' I thanked him and hung up. I thought, what exactly does she have to do, sir, before someone does something? Are you going to ring me up when she dies of a drug overdose and tell me, 'Mrs Wunderle, we have found your daughter. She's dead.'

I was furious. I had heart palpitations. I always liked to have control of things, but all this had left me powerless. We were all out on a limb, left hanging, ready to fall.

Two nights later, after reporting her as a missing person again, I was sitting in my favourite chair—the one covered in Sanderson linen with the big cabbage roses over it. I was wrapped in my towelling dressing-gown and all ready to go to bed. The phone rang. I said, 'That'll be Kartya.' Josh answered it. He said, 'Mum, it's the police.' I jumped up and answered it. The voice on the end said, 'Mrs Wunderle, this is Sergeant Jeffries from Dandenong Police Station. We have your daughter Kartya here. We will charge her with possession and use of a drug of dependence. Would you come down while we interview her?' I said, 'Yes, I'll be there as soon as I can.'

It was 11 o'clock at night. I got dressed and got in my car and drove for 45 minutes to Dandenong. I walked in to the police station and gave Kartya a hug. She didn't look very well. We went into an interview room where the sergeant recorded the interview. He asked her how long she'd been using heroin, where she got it from and where she was living. After he'd finished, he said, 'I will be charging you with possession and use of a drug of dependence. You will receive a summons to go to court and you'll probably just get a good behaviour bond.' He asked Kartya, 'Do you want to get off the heroin?' She said, 'Of course I do, but how?' He said, 'Just stop using it.' 'Sure,' she said. 'It's not that easy.'

I said to him, 'You're charging my daughter with possession and use of a drug of dependence. What does that tell you? She's not a criminal, she has a medical problem.' He was very sympathetic, but he said that the law states that the use of heroin is a criminal offence. She had committed a crime. He didn't need me to tell him that the system was wrong, he said. 'Tell the politicians. I have to deal with this every day and it's very sad.'

I asked him, 'Where can we go to help her get off it?' He shrugged his shoulders and said, 'Nowhere, Mrs Wunderle. There really is nowhere. Maybe you can try Odyssey House.'

The next morning Kartya was still saying that she really did want to get off the heroin and that she needed us to help her. I rang Odyssey House and asked them if they would take her. They said they would, but only after she had detoxed. I said, 'What's the point of that? How's she supposed to detox?' The counsellor told me to find an understanding doctor and he would give her medication to help her through it.

I made an appointment at the local medical centre, our own family doctor had moved to the country. I took Kartya along. She was still saying that she really wanted to get off the heroin. We went into the doctor's waiting room before finally being called in to see him. He was a tall, thin man with glasses. He looked about fifty-five years old. He asked Kartya, 'How can I help you, young lady?' Kartya said, 'I am using heroin and I need something to help me get off it.' His eyes darted in my direction, 'Who are you?' he said. I replied, 'I'm Kartya's mother.' 'Then how can you allow her to use heroin?' I felt like he was blaming me. I answered sarcastically, 'And how would you suggest I stop her, Doctor?'

He didn't answer me. He prescribed medication for Kartya and said that I had to administer the tablets. He said, 'If they don't work, you can always go on methadone.' Kartya said, 'Sure, that's fucking addictive too.'

We got up to leave, and on the way out he said, 'You should

wake up to yourself, young lady.' He looked at me, and said, 'If they don't work, don't bring her back here again.' I turned and looked at him. I thought, you stupid old man. I said, 'Don't worry, Doctor, we won't be back. And, by the way, thanks. Thanks for nothing.'

My stomach was churning, my heart was thumping. I was biting my bottom lip and shaking my head. Kartya said, 'See, Mum, everyone thinks I'm just a fucking junkie.' I said, 'We don't, Kartya. We don't.' We went home to detox.

Othmar and I made up a bed for Kartya in our room. We put a mattress on the floor so we could keep an eye on her. Besides, she didn't want to be on her own. She was scared. She groaned and writhed around her bed all night. We didn't sleep at all. It was terrible. She was in so much pain and we didn't know what to do. We gave her the medication. It helped, but she was deeply depressed. We were more worried about her depression than the heroin.

I continued to try and find a drug rehabilitation program for Kartya to participate in. I wasn't sure that detoxing at home was the answer because we didn't know what to do afterwards. I rang every major hospital in Melbourne to enquire about a program. Finally someone told me about St Vincent's Hospital. I phoned straight away, and was told, yes, they had a program. I thought, fantastic. I've finally found somewhere. They connected me to the drug unit. I explained that my daughter was addicted to heroin; could they help us? The gentleman on the phone sounded very sympathetic and understanding. He said I was doing the right thing, and that a program was the most successful way of beating the addiction. He said they had one vacancy and that Kartya could start in the next few days. I was elated. He asked for details, such as name, address and so on. Then he said, 'Oh, by the way, Mrs

Wunderle, how old is Kartya?' I said, 'She's just turned sixteen.' Then he said, 'I'm sorry, very sorry, but we can't accept her.' I couldn't believe my ears when he said, 'She's too young. Our cut-off age is eighteen.'

'You have to be joking, surely,' I said. He said he wasn't joking and that they were not geared to treat someone so young. He was very sorry and he could not recommend anywhere else in Victoria. He said there was a really good program in New South Wales if we could get her up there.

I thanked him and hung up. I was furious, flabbergasted and absolutely dumbfounded. I couldn't for the life of me understand why there was not a program available to someone Kartya's age in the state of Victoria. Where did we live, the North Pole?

I sat down and wrote a letter to the premier and to our local member of parliament. I got no acknowledgement from either of them. It made us wonder who really cared. Nobody seemed interested in a family with a young person enslaved by drugs. A social worker friend told me that there was a possibility that a drug rehabilitation unit was to be opened up in Dandenong, but that could be a year or so away. What do we do in the meantime? We couldn't understand why a young person with an addiction was treated so differently to a young person with a physical illness. To us, addiction was an illness. If your child is physically ill, you can take them to a hospital and get treatment to make them well. If your child is emotionally ill, then bad luck, because you can't take them to a hospital for treatment. If you're unlucky, they may get picked up by the police, charged with possession and use of a drug of dependence and get a good behaviour bond.

I use a drug of dependence every day by smoking. I've tried to give it up and failed every time, so why is it so hard for people to understand that when a young person becomes addicted to heroin, it's not that simple to get off it? Why does society treat them with such contempt? Why do we make them feel worse than they already do? Why are they referred to as junkies and considered society's losers? Why aren't we, as parents, given more support by the medical profession to help our kids? Why should we have to ring a medical centre and ask if they have a doctor on duty who will treat a person with an addiction? When will our society wake up and realise just how many of our young people are affected by drug addiction? The average person would not have a clue about the number of very young people using heroin. The stigma attached to heroin addiction is a tragedy.

One day when I was out on the streets of Springvale looking for Kartya, I met a young girl called Susanna. She was only fourteen years old. She told me her parents were Polish. She looked sad and lonely and she was stoned. I asked her if I could help her. She said she needed money for food. I told her that I wouldn't give her money, but that I would buy her some food. We went to a takeaway food shop and we bought a salad roll and some chips. I sat down outside with her while she wolfed down the food and I asked her why she wasn't at school. She told me that she had been using heroin for three months and her parents had told her to leave home and not come back until she was off it. She was the eldest of four children. She said that she could not stop using heroin because all her friends were using it. One of them had died from an overdose. She was living with friends in an abandoned Housing Commission house in Noble Park. I gave her a business card from Wesley Youth Services and told her to ring them if she needed help.

This poor young girl was just a baby, abandoned by her family, left alone without any love or support to help her through her problems. I was determined that Kartya would never feel that we had given up on her. I didn't find Kartya, but as I drove home, I wept for Susanna. I wept for all the Susannas out there who nobody cared about.

We succeeded in detoxing Kartya at home. She stayed for a few weeks, put on weight and, for a time, returned to her normal self. Her network of friends was continually ringing and eventually seduced her back, away from us, her family. She left us to continue to worry about her. Othmar and I both knew that she would start using heroin again. Her illness was addiction. You can't cure that with a few tablets. As she left, I made her promise that she would contact me every second day and, if she needed anything, to let us know. She promised me that she would. We were supporting her financially, giving her money to survive. At least that way we knew she had money for food. Kartya couldn't go without her Chinese food, we knew that, so we knew some of the money did go to feed herself.

She wouldn't stay at home with us; she was afraid that the fights would start again and her anger would get out of control. The only thing she could control was the fact that she could just leave and remove herself from what she saw as her failure to live up to our expectations. She could see that her actions were causing everyone in the family distress and she was unable to do anything about it. No matter how hard she tried, nothing went right for her. Everything just fell apart. Every time the brick wall that she had built around herself started to fall down, she bolted. She didn't want to leave herself vulnerable. She was carrying enough pain to fill ten suitcases; our pain was the last thing she wanted to deal with.

We tried to understand Kartya's addiction to heroin by finding out as much as we could about the effects of the drug and the reasons particular people feel the need to use it to get through their lives. Heroin takes away pain. Kartya was certainly experiencing deep emotional pain and anguish. The effect of heroin is to make problems seem to disappear. A person can become addicted to heroin in a matter of weeks. It is one of the most addictive drugs known, both physically and mentally. When a person becomes addicted, they need the drug daily in order to remain normal. Once a person withdraws from heroin and the physical dependence has ended, often a more insidious condition remains, that is the mental addiction; the craving for the drug can persist long after the body is free of it. It can take many attempts to withdraw before a person is completely cured.

Often a person addicted to heroin has low self-esteem, feelings of incompetence and hopelessness. It is not uncommon, either, for them to have an unusual attachment and become strangely dependent upon one family member, even though they may abuse that person, and give the general impression that they dislike them.

An addicted person usually suffers from repressed or hidden feelings of anger and guilt. Absence of parental love in childhood can leave extreme feelings of grief and abandonment. Heroin soothes these feelings and gives the addicted person a feeling of warmth and comfort; it suppresses the pain and anger.

These were all the feelings that Kartya was experiencing. Her continual need to test my love for her was evident in the way she related to me. She knew that I loved her unconditionally, but continually created situations where she believed I could change my mind if I wanted.

CHAPTER EIGHTEEN
A Death in the Family

My mother died. She wasn't supposed to; she was supposed to get sick and then get better. Not die. I still needed her to be here. I still had more questions to ask her. I wasn't ready for her to die, not yet. Perfect mothers just don't die. They don't just go to sleep and not wake up. Did she have to die now? Couldn't she wait a bit longer until we didn't need her any more? Why did she have to die when we all still needed her? I felt like somebody had shot me; shot me through the heart and the blood had filled my body till I couldn't breathe anymore. I felt like a bus had run over me and left me splattered on the ground. Who would I ring now for support? Nobody will say that I look like my mother any more because she's gone.

Maybe she just got tired at the end of her journey. She had reached her destination. She was too tired to go on.

She was so beautiful when she died. I held her lovely soft hands.

Her nails were manicured. I stroked her cheeks and told her that I loved her. She knew all her kids loved her. My mother taught me everything about unconditional love. She had left me with the greatest gift of all. Through her example she had taught me to never give in. To never give up on what you believe in. I never thought she would die; I thought she would always be there. Now that she'd gone, I thought of all the things I wanted to tell her, all the things I wanted to ask her. But I couldn't, because she had died.

Dear Diary,

My nan is dying. I've never known anyone in my family to die. When my nan dies, something in my mum will be gone. I hate seeing my mum upset. Mum, you can be strong, I know you can. I love you, Mum.

Kartya

Maybe I could ask my dad. He would be all alone now. He would advise me, I knew he would. I told him I loved him. I was fifty-one when I told him for the very first time. I just came straight out with it. I said, 'Dad, I love you.' He said, 'I love you too, darling.' It was a load off my shoulders because I had always wanted to tell him but I just couldn't spit it out. It was easy after that. I always said I loved him from then on.

When we buried my mum, I'd never felt so close to anyone in my whole life as I did to my brothers and sisters at that moment. We all shared each other's loss. We all knew how we were feeling. In a way, we all still needed our mother. I was glad that I wasn't an only child. I couldn't imagine going through that pain without my brothers and sisters.

It took me a long time to get used to the fact that I couldn't just pick up the phone and talk to my mum. I would talk to her in my mind, but it wasn't the same. Nothing would ever be the same again.

Weeks went by before we saw Kartya again. Every couple of days, usually at ridiculous hours of the night and early morning, she would ring. I was always getting out of bed to answer the phone. If it was after ten at night, I always knew it was her. I would always ask her if she had any plans to come home. She would just say, 'No, Mum, I can't.' When I asked ask her why, she would just say, 'Mum, I can't. I just can't.' I would ask her if she was all right, if she was taking care of herself. I would always tell her that we loved her and that we would like her to come home. When I would ask her where she was living, she would say, 'with friends'. She would never tell us where. When it was midwinter, cold and wet, I couldn't understand why she didn't want to come home, where it was warm and dry.

Many times, Othmar and I found ourselves going off to look for her. We would get in the car and drive to Springvale. We thought we saw her often, but it was never her, just another person on the streets who looked like her.

One night Othmar arrived home from work. He always caught the last train from the city. He said he thought he saw Kartya. There was a girl lying on the steps of Flinders Street station in a sleeping bag. She had a hood over her head and she was asleep. He told me he stood there for about fifteen minutes until she turned her head. She didn't have a beauty spot beside her eye; he knew then it wasn't Kartya.

I spent hours on the phone ringing Child Protection, Juvenile Justice and Kartya's social worker, asking them all the same questions. Have they heard from or seen Kartya? Isn't there something they can do to make Kartya come home? The answers were always the same: if she doesn't want to come home, no-one can make her.

I had Kartya's phone diary with over one hundred phone numbers in it. I rang them all, but they didn't seem to know where she was living, at least that's what they told me. We couldn't compete with this network she had. They had all become her family. She didn't seem to need us any more. I rang my friend Pam nearly every day. We've been friends for nearly twenty years. She is an adoptive mother of a son and daughter from the Philippines. I must have driven her crazy. Sometimes, out of frustration and anger I cried like a big sook. She kept me sane. She was a social worker and one of my best friends. She was always positive and supportive. She didn't put Kartya down. She told me that we were doing the right thing and to keep hanging in there. Some nights, I drank until I was quite drunk. It soothed the pain of the growth in my stomach, the one that had knotted up my insides. It blotted out reality and also made me feel normal. My empathy and understanding for Kartya was growing daily as we both carried our different bags of pain. When she didn't ring us I got myself in quite a state, couldn't eat, couldn't sleep, couldn't concentrate on anything.

I waited for the police to knock on the door and tell me she had overdosed.

I felt so alone, as if we were the only family in the world going through this. I screamed out silently: Can't somebody help us? Can't anyone see that we are all falling apart? Kartya's life was totally out of control. Kiersten, Alex and Josh all wanted to leave home. I understood how they felt. I wanted to leave, too. How to keep us all together? I stopped communicating with some of my best friends. They had told me to forget about Kartya, that she was not worth it. I didn't want to hear any negative stuff, so I cut myself off.

I decided that if we were going to survive this, then I had to cope. If I gave up on her, then everyone else would too. Othmar and I sat down with the kids and made it clear to them that we all had to stick together, otherwise it would destroy us.

We couldn't change the path that Kartya was on, we could only change the way we looked at it. Otherwise we would lose her. They did not want that. They loved her, they just wanted her better. There was no way that she was going to allow herself to be loved by us, that would be too risky for her: what if we rejected or abandoned her? She fought against our love as if her life depended on it. She was screaming out silently for us to hear her. We saw and felt her pain, but felt powerless to help her. We had to stand by and watch while a beautiful young person slowly destroyed herself. We would find an answer. We would find a way to take away the pain. I just didn't know when and I didn't know how.

Somehow I felt the answer lay in her rejection of me. Her anger towards me was unnatural. She was angry with me all the time. Every time she told me that she hated me, I would tell her that I loved her. She had this need to ring me, talk to me, abuse me and then hang up. I couldn't help but feel that all this anger was indirectly meant for her birth mother. I had posted over fifty letters to people I didn't even know, all names and addresses I got out of the Taiwanese phone book. Only by finding this birth mother could we start to put the puzzle together. I asked in the letters if they could find somebody for us; if they would help us find Lin-Ah-Hua. I never got an answer from anyone. I was feeling as if this birth mother didn't even exist. We had to keep trying, we had to. We had no other choice.

CHAPTER NINETEEN
Locked Up

One night I went to our local supermarket. It was about 11.30 p.m. I had been working all day and I was tired and stressed. Nothing unusual for me. I walked up and down with my trolley. Suddenly, I spotted Kartya down the end of the store. I froze. My initial reaction was to run away. I was afraid to see her because I thought that she would just scream at me and abuse me. She was with a feral-looking young boy. I quickly paid for my groceries and walked out of the shop and waited for her to appear. She was surprised to see me. I asked her if she wanted to come home for the night. She looked unwell and scruffy. She asked me who was at home and I told her that Kiersten and Josh were there. She said no, that she didn't want to come home. I could tell that she felt guilty and didn't want to face the other kids. I put my arms around her and gave her a hug. She pulled away quickly. I told her that we loved her. Two days later, I got a letter from her.

Dear Mum, It hurts me so much inside to see you like this, when you looked so exhausted I didn't know what to do or say to you. I was so scared and frightened. I suppose all I can say is that I am truly sorry for the things I have put the family through. I know I say I hate you and that you are not my real mother, but deep down inside, I really do love you and you are my real mother. I know this and always have. You are the one who brought me up from a baby. When you got me, you treated and cared for me as if I was your own, and I am your real daughter deep down inside. I don't mean to hurt you like I do, and I'm sure you know this. I don't mean to be the rebellious little bitch that I am. In fact, I'm not even sure why I do these things that I have done over the past few years. Maybe as Dad said, it's psychological, because of what happened to me in the first nine months of my life. I remember when Dad told me, I went to my room and cried. I didn't cry because of what happened to me, I cried because of the love and care you gave me. You both loved me so much and you still do, that's why I cried, because I have treated you all so bad. I have been the cause of you having breakdowns or whatever it was. Please don't say that it isn't my fault, because I know it is. I am not asking for your forgiveness, but because of the pain I have bought on the family, I am asking for your continuous love and support. I know you will keep on loving and caring for me, I just want to make sure you will love me forever. I know you would have preferred me to say this to you both personally, but you know I can't say this face to face. All I can say is, this is from my heart, I love you Mum and Dad, always and forever.

Mum, when you hugged me the other night, I didn't want to let go, but I had to. When I saw my friend later on that night, I couldn't stop crying because you looked so run down and so sad. Please Mum, just love me and stick by me.

Always your daughter, Kartya.

I cried when I read that letter. I really did believe that she loved us and she felt that her only option was to sort out her life on her own, away from us. I wanted to bring her home and force her to face the demons that haunted her, but I couldn't. All I could do was make sure I kept tabs on her wherever she went. To continue to try and hang on to her.

Weeks later, Kartya rang Othmar and me at about 12.30 at night. She said, 'Mum, can you come and get me. I want to come home.' I asked her where she was and she told me she was standing at a phone box in the main street of Springvale. Othmar and I left straight away to bring her home. As we drove towards her, she looked a tragic figure, standing there in the dark, all on her own with just the clothes she stood up in. I asked her what had happened and she just said, 'My friends kicked me out.' I said, 'Kartya, where is your bag and all your clothes?' She said, 'I've lost them, Mum. I left them at friends' houses and lost them all.' I shook my head and uttered a sigh of relief that at least she was still standing up and breathing. That's all that mattered. Nothing else.

We took our daughter home, made her something to eat and put her to bed. The other kids were happy she was home, but a bit sceptical that it would last. She was trying to be nice to them, but they were cautious. They were waiting for the worm to turn. She told us that she hadn't been using heroin for a while. We believed her because she didn't appear stoned. She told us that Tran was soon to be released from the youth detention centre. We felt that she would probably go straight back to him but, of course, we hoped that she would stay at home and sort out her life.

At times she almost seemed happy at home with all of us. She would go in the kitchen and cook her own food. The house would smell like a Chinese restaurant. Some days she would go out and not come back until the next day, but we were grateful that at least she did come back. We bought her new clothes to replace the lost ones. Financially this one child was costing us more than the other three put together. Kartya told us that a new drug rehabilitation unit had opened up in Dandenong. A friend of hers was trying to get in, but there was a five-week waiting list. I couldn't help but think how ridiculous that situation was. When a young person wants to detox they have to be able to do it straight away. A lot can happen in five weeks. Anyway, I was fairly confident that we wouldn't be needing to utilise the service. With a bit of luck, Kartya would stay clean. She was seeing her psychologist and we were hoping that she was talking about her problems. But she still had a huge anger problem and appeared to be suffering from occasional, but deep, depression. We worried she was suicidal. When I read a poem that she had written and left on her floor, it worried both Othmar and me.

Say Goodbye

I'm crying out inside, to end this life of sadness.
So lonely, so afraid, to live my life alone.
My tears, no-one can see,
How do I break free from this loneliness?
I can't go on another day.
How do I make things right?
My heart and soul are left behind
Where do I find them?
Every day and every night, I have feelings of desire
to say goodbye
Where do I go from now?
Should I just say goodbye?

Kartya

The salubrious facade of the big old two-storey, ochre-painted Victorian-style building, with bars on the windows, gave no indication as to what was inside. Nestled amongst other well-to-do homes in a leafy tree-lined street in one of the better suburbs of Melbourne, it could have been home to any normal average family. But the family inside this house was quite different. It was a temporary home for six out-of-control female adolescents. One of them was our daughter, coerced there by her psychologist at my insistence; locked up in secure welfare to keep her out of harm's way.

We had let go of the tiger by the tail momentarily. The tiger upped and left, back on to the streets, with the drugs, the so-called friends and a lifestyle that was unacceptable to this bewildered, frustrated, exhausted, average Australian family. I had enlisted the help of Child Protection. I rang them and said, 'Isn't there anything you can do?' I begged them to do something. We couldn't do anything. We had no idea where she had gone. I went out one day and came home to find her bag and clothes gone. No note. She had an appointment with her psychologist that day. Sometimes she went, sometimes she didn't. I spoke to her probation officer and she said, 'Really, Nola, all we can do is lock her up; get a court order and put her in secure accommodation.' My reply was, 'Well, do it. Find her and lock her up.'

So our daughter was locked up. For the next ten days I slept like a baby, secure in the knowledge that she was safe—not on the streets and not taking drugs. At first she was angry with me, very angry. She called me names that weren't even in the dictionary. Then, after the first few days, it was as if she was happy to be there. She seemed quite content making craft things that she would give me when I went to visit her. I would drive over to see her every day and take her some special treats. I would go in the big locked front doors and get searched before I could go into the main section of the house. Kartya and I would go outside together for a cigarette. She would make me laugh when she would say, 'Mum, all the other girls are fucked in the head.' She never saw herself to be like them, this big, tough street kid, with the foul mouth and the aggressive out-of-control temper. We didn't, either, because we knew somewhere inside this person was a sweet, caring, intelligent, well-mannered young lady with a wicked sense of humour. We hoped that she would emerge in our midst soon.

At least with her locked up in Windsor House I had no need to put into action the vivid dream that I had had two nights before. I was in a big hardware store and they had this heavy brass chain on a big roll. I dreamt that I bought three metres of it and a big padlock with a key. I went home and, when Kartya was asleep, I put the chain around her ankle and padlocked the other end to her bed. The chain was just long enough to reach the bathroom and toilet. When I woke up next morning, I had a smile on my face.

I knew I couldn't do it, but I wished to hell that I could.

When Kartya was released from secure accommodation, she came home for two days. The kids had a huge fight. They confronted Kartya when I was at work. They told her everything that had built up inside them, how they couldn't live with her while she continued to hurt us all. She couldn't take it, so she packed her bag and left. She went to live at Tran's house. When I saw her a week later, she was using heroin again. Kartya said she didn't want to see any of us for a while, but she promised me that she would ring me and let us know that she was all right.

CHAPTER TWENTY
Detox, Again

We didn't see Kartya for two months. She lived with Tran in the garage at the back of his mother's house. Every time I rang, she was either asleep or not there. My attitude was a bit like out of sight, try and get her out of mind. We were all exhausted. I didn't really want her back home until she could face her addiction and do something permanent about it. We all needed to survive. The other kids deserved some peace from the madness in our lives. Josh asked me every day: 'Have you heard from Kartya?'

She rang every other day, mostly late at night. I think she and her friends slept all day and stayed up all night. I always asked her how she was and she always told me she was fine. I didn't believe her. I asked her if I could come and see her and she always said no. I threatened her that I would ring Child Protection if she didn't let us see her. Half of me wanted to see her, the other half didn't. I could only guess at what she would be like; how angry and aggressive she would be. I was scared for her, and I just wouldn't get it into my head that I couldn't help her.

After a lot of pleading, one day she relented, and agreed to go out for dinner with Othmar and me. We told her that she could bring Tran, but she didn't want to. She thought we blamed him for her addiction, but we didn't. We picked her up and went to a restaurant for dinner. She looked very thin and not very well. At least she looked clean and she was well dressed. She had just used, we could tell by her mood. She was edgy and aggressive. We tried not to be critical. We just chitchatted with her. We were sitting at the table and I was looking at her. I couldn't take my eyes off her. I hadn't seen her for months. I couldn't help it, I just wanted to look at her. She said, 'Mum, what the fuck are you looking at?' I answered, 'Kartya, can't I just look at you? I haven't seen you for so long.' She said, 'Yeah, sure, but you look stupid, sitting there looking at me for no reason.' I took my eyes off her, and we got up to get something to eat. When we sat down at the table again, I scratched the end of my nose. She got very abusive with me and said, 'Mum, that's why I don't want to go out with you. You just sit at the table and pick your nose.' I told her that I wasn't picking, just scratching. She swore and cursed at me for the rest of the evening, telling me what bad manners I had. If Othmar hadn't kicked my leg under the table, it could have ended in World War Three. I decided to keep my mouth shut, and didn't scratch my nose for the rest of the evening, even though it was itchy. I sat there with a smile on my face, shaking my head.

It was about five more weeks before we saw her again. I would ring her but she would just say, 'Mum, I don't want to see you or Dad.' I could have understood it if she didn't want to see me, but the fact that she didn't want to see Othmar made me think that all was not well. Finally, I couldn't stand it any more, so I took the day off work and drove over to Tran's house. I was prepared for a confrontation. His sister answered the door. She invited me in and I sat down. I told her that I had to see Kartya, that it was urgent. She went out of the room. Ten minutes later she returned and said that Kartya didn't want to see me. She told me to go home. I said that if she didn't come to see me, I would go out to the garage and get her. After some time, Kartya came in. She could hardly walk, she was like a stick. She sat down beside me and I could see her hip bones sticking out. She looked anorexic. My stomach turned over, my heart started thumping. I put my arms around her and we both started crying. I screamed at Tran's mother, who was standing watching. She couldn't speak English. 'Why didn't you tell us she was so sick?' I yelled. I said, 'Damn you all. I'm taking her to hospital.'

Kartya looked at me with her sad eyes, and said, 'Mum, I'm not going with you. I'm staying here.' I told her that I wasn't moving. I would stay there until she came with me, even if it took all day and all night. I was not leaving without her. I sat there for hours, crying, begging, pleading with her. I screamed at Tran, 'Why don't you make her come with me?' He just shook his head. I think he thought that if she got off heroin, he would lose her. She told me she couldn't eat. Every time she ate, she threw up. So she just stopped eating. I knew that if I left without her, she would die.

Eventually she decided to come with me. I half carried her to the car, she could hardly walk. I told her that I was taking her straight to the new detox unit in Dandenong. She agreed, and told me that she and Tran had both booked to go in, but there was a two-week waiting list. They wanted to detox together. She said, 'Thanks, Mum, I really wanted to come, but I'm worried about Tran.' I told her that I understood, but that we needed to get her well before we could think of anyone else. I knew that she badly wanted to get off the drugs, but her addiction was so heavy it had her totally in its grip.

She vomited twice in the car on the way. I wondered if we were going to make it. When we arrived, I ran in and told them that my daughter was in the car, she was unable to walk and was very ill; could they admit her straight away? An efficient middle-aged woman said, 'I'm sorry, but we don't have any vacancies. Besides, we have a two-week wait.' I went crazy. I screamed, 'My daughter's in the fucking car half dead and you're telling me you won't fucking take her?' I felt like I would have a heart attack on the spot. I threatened to ring every television station and expose the inadequacies of a system that turns away a sixteen-year-old girl who wants to get off heroin.

Where the hell were we supposed to go? Did she have to die before anyone would help us? I hated everyone. I hated the system that didn't work. I hated the politicians who weren't listening to our kids. I hated the adults who made the drug accessible to our daughter and to everyone else's children. I felt like I wanted to drive off the West Gate Bridge and end everyone's pain. Kartya was devastated. She started crying, 'Mum, what happens now?' I said, 'I don't know, Kartya, but I know one thing, you're not going to fucking die on us. We'll help you, we'll fix it, I promise you that.'

I asked her to come back home with me but she wouldn't and I knew why. One night without heroin and she would go nuts. I drove her home and fed her, then took her back to Tran's house. As I opened the car door to help her out, she said to me, 'Mum, do you think we'll ever find my birth mother?' I looked at her and said, 'Kartya, I promise you now that as soon as we can, we will find her. That I promise.' I knew that until we found her mother, then none of this was going to go away. She was consumed by the need to find her. For some inexplicable reason, she was tied to her birth mother. We had to find her, otherwise Kartya would die.

I prayed all night that she wouldn't overdose. I felt so guilty that I had not gone to see her before. I should have known that when she didn't want to see us that there was something wrong. I was angry with myself. I vowed that from then on I would see her every day. When Othmar got home from work, I told him what had happened. He looked so sad. He loved her so much and felt so powerless to help her. The next day I got a call from the detox unit to say that they would admit Kartya immediately. I thought, thank God for that.

Kiersten went and picked Kartya up and took her to the unit. I warned Kiersten how bad Kartya looked, but I knew that no matter what I said, nothing was going to prepare her for what she was to encounter. When Kiersten got home that night, she broke down and said, 'Mum, she looks terrible. I don't want to see my sister like that.' I put my arms around her and we both cried. I thought to myself how each member of a family with an addictive person is so affected. Everyone, in a way, becomes a co-dependent. Yet in spite of it, we were all still very close. We all just wanted it over with and for us to get back to being a normal family.

We were all relieved that Kartya was in detox. We were hopeful that she would get well, but after two days it all got too much for her. She felt scared and alone with only adult male alcoholics as her fellow patients. She was having no counselling, only medication. She rang and begged me to come and get her. I brought her home not really knowing what we were going to do. She was still deeply depressed and we had all got to the stage where we didn't know how we could help her. It was a terrible feeling of hopelessness.

I went out and bought myself a new jacket. It was Thai silk with every colour of the rainbow sewn together like patchwork. I put it on. It made me feel better, it put a smile on my face. It didn't help Kartya, but it helped me to look forward to the next day because, whether I liked it or not, tomorrow was going to come and it had to be dealt with. My technicolour jacket would make the day easier to get through. At least I would look like I was having a good time.

Help Me

I look at you now,
you're just skin and bones
from a disease that takes
and gives nothing back
This world of drugs, has taken you away
left us with nothing, we can say
We tried our best, but in the end
you made your choice
left us with nothing to mend
Took yourself away from the love we had
Gave us no choice, left us feeling bad

Love was never enough for you
after all the pain you went through
You threw it all away and just gave up
and left us without a thread of hope
But if you think we've given up
then think again
We're not prepared to walk away
from one we love, without a fight
Tomorrow will bring another day

CHAPTER TWENTY-ONE
Pain

𝓘 found an essay Kartya had written. When I read it, it made me realise how depressed she was. It was, supposedly, fictional.

That was the First Moment at Which I Started to Realise What True Courage Was

When I looked down at the pavement, I was so shocked at what I saw. It was my lifeless body. I was dead, but somehow I knew I was not dreaming because it felt so real, being out of my body and being replaced as a spirit of some kind.

I must have fainted, well, I mean, my spirit, because when I woke up, I wasn't where I had fainted. I was at my family's home in Mitcham. It must have been about eight o'clock in the morning. My whole family was up and about, doing their usual things, having breakfast and getting dressed. That's when the phone rang.

I ran for it, as usual, and tried to answer it, but my hand just swiped through the phone, then I remembered, I was dead. My brother, Josh answered it, 'Hello, yes, I'll just get her for you . . . Mum, it's for you.' My mum came over to the phone. 'Hello,' my mum said. She was listening to the person on the other end of the phone. It must have been the police telling her about me, because she started crying, 'Yes, I'll be there soon,' she answered. She hung up the phone and sat there for twenty minutes crying. My brother came out of his room and saw my mother crying. 'Mum, what's wrong?' he asked. 'Kartya's dead,' she replied. My brother told my dad and my sister. They were so upset by my death that I had to just get out of the house. I ran all the way to my best friend, Misty's house. She was in her bedroom. She must have been told about my death, because she was crying and yelling out, 'Kartya, why? Why did you leave me?'

My funeral passed, and everything seemed to settle down slowly. Except for Misty, she was taking things really bad, after all we had been best friends for six years. She must have been crying, because her eyes were all puffy and red. It was about ten o'clock at night, I had just left Misty's house. I was walking down the street, when this shadow of the same size and appearance of me appeared out of nowhere. It must have known I was there, because it started walking slowly towards me. As it came closer, its face was really terrifying, so I ran for it. I ran as fast as I could down Misty's street. I looked back and it was still coming towards me. I just kept running and running. I didn't know where to turn, so I turned into what must have been an alley, as it came to a dead end. The shadow came closer and closer and I tried to scream, but no-one could hear or see me. It must have known who I was, because it wasn't rough with me. I was trying my hardest to fight it off, when it eventually overpowered me and won. It knocked me unconscious. I started seeing my past, from when I was a tiny baby, until the day I died. It was showing me about my life and how I was raised and how I treated those who loved me, it even showed me the time I was really bad on drugs. I guess it was the drugs that made me jump, I must have been really depressed about life that I had no way of getting out of the world of drugs. That's why I took the easy way out and committed suicide. I woke up at my family's house and that was the first moment at which I started to realise what true courage was . . . just by facing The Shadow, I was no longer afraid . . .

We all knew that Kartya was still using heroin. It was something we all lived with. Most of the time she was all right; sometimes she got quite aggressive. We were used to the slamming doors, her getting furious over nothing. We accepted that that was Kartya; after six years, we were used to it. I still wrote letters to Taiwan to find Lin-Ah-Hua: the birth mother of all birth mothers. I couldn't wait to find her. Was I going to give her a piece of my mind! With a bit of luck, she might want her back. I smiled to myself, thinking, 'I don't think so, Nola.' Anyway, Kartya wouldn't be going anywhere until she got well again, and that wouldn't happen until Kartya decided so for herself.

One thing we had learnt: you can't order someone to stop an addiction, no matter what that addiction is.

We didn't think Kartya actually used heroin at home. We hadn't asked her. It was still pretty scary stuff for us. It was not as if she was going to sit down and have a big family heart-to-heart meeting about it. If we wanted her to leave that would have been a sure way of getting her to do a runner. She'd be gone like a shot if we called a family conference. We'd rather have her home as a live person addicted to heroin, than a dead person on the street, with no-one. That way we could make sure she was eating and in general looking after herself.

A once-upon-a-time friend of mine said to me that she thought we were stupid letting her live at home when she was using heroin. She said that would encourage her to use it more. I tried to explain to her that it didn't work that way. I said to her, 'It all depends on how much guilt you're prepared to live with if something happened.' She said she wouldn't feel at all guilty. If it was her kid, she would kick her out. I told her that I didn't agree with her, and that sort of attitude gave me the shits. I never saw her again. I don't think she liked me any more. I wished Kartya would hurry up and get well. I didn't have all that many friends left.

When we were feeling depressed about the journey Kartya was travelling, we would go back to the reasons why we loved her in the first place. We would get out the family photo albums to remind ourselves that we had all been a happy family at one stage in our lives. There is nothing like having an addicted person in the family to make you feel like a failure as a parent. Othmar and I would go through all the 'what if ' scenarios. We never came up with any answer that we felt would have made a difference. We tried to focus on the fact that Kartya's strong independent spirit, her bombastic personality, was all part of her nature; that for some reason in the future she would need those qualities.

Because she had difficulty communicating with us about what was happening with her emotions and feelings, we would write letters to her. I would give them to her or leave them on her bed. I would pick out funny cards sometimes and write on them. We would tell her how we felt; we would tell her that what she was doing was hurting us but, despite all that, we loved her and would continue to support her. I know that way of communicating with her helped, because she would write letters back to us, conveying her feelings. She would have never sat down and talked to us the way she wrote to us in her letters.

We wanted to be able to still have a good relationship with her when this was all over. In a strange sort of way, though, we did all still have a good relationship, although at times it was fragile.

I had been having trouble sleeping, so I went to the doctor and she gave me something to help me sleep. I would take this little yellow tablet, put my head on the pillow and within minutes I would be asleep. It was heaven to be able to sleep through the night. The doctor told me that they were non-habit forming, so I was confident that when my sleeping pattern was established, I wouldn't need to take them any more. One night, I couldn't find them. I'd forgotten where I'd put them. I was beside myself. I looked in every corner of the house. I had the kids looking everywhere, Othmar was looking everywhere, nobody could find them. All I could think was that I was not going to be able to sleep. Eventually I found them in the rubbish bin. I'd thrown the box out with some other rubbish. I sat down and cried. I cried because I'd found them and I cried because I had become dependent on them.

I did take one that night, but the next morning I threw them all in the bin. I wouldn't be needing them any more. I was beginning to understand our daughter more and more. How could I, as an adult, judge my daughter when I had obviously become addicted to a little yellow tablet without even being aware of it? I only realised my problem when I couldn't find them. The day I put hair gel on my face instead of my anti-wrinkle cream, I seriously questioned my sanity. When I told the kids what I had done, they had this look in their eyes that said, 'Oh, my God, she's lost it.' My excuse was that both the jars looked the same to me without my glasses on. The kids didn't believe me, but Othmar did. Although he did point out to me that the jar with the hair gel in it was black and the face cream jar was pink and white. The last straw came when I got ready for work one day, got in my car and when I was halfway there, realised that it was my day off. I returned home and when the kids asked me why, I just said that I felt sick. I didn't tell them that I'd forgotten it was my day off. I didn't have the courage. I didn't even tell Othmar.

One morning I was getting ready to go to work. I'd had my shower, washed my hair, put in my hot rollers and I was walking around in my big fluffy towelling dressing-gown. Kartya was in her room. Othmar and the other kids were all at work. I was going to make a cup of tea. I called out to Kartya, 'Do you want a cup of tea?' She didn't answer. I knocked on her door and opened it. She was squatting on the floor with a belt around her arm and a syringe in her hand. I freaked. I hadn't actually ever seen her do it before. I don't know why I screamed—it's not as if I should have been shocked. It was just seeing her do it. I started to feel faint and I had chest pains. Kartya went nuts and flew out of her room. On the way out she pushed me out of her way and I fell against the glass door. I dropped to the floor. I lay on the floor, begging her not to go. She walked over the top of me and ran out of the door screaming. I couldn't get up.

Next thing I knew, an ambulance siren was blaring out the front of the house. There was a knock on the door but I didn't open it. I talked through the door. The ambulance officer asked me to open the door. I was still on the floor. I opened it an inch and he asked if he could come in. I said, 'No, I've got my hair in rollers.' After I said it, I thought what a stupid thing to say.

He said, 'I'm sorry, madam, but you must let us in.' I opened the door and let them both in. I assured them that I was all right. They said they had a call from a Kartya to come and check her mum, because she'd fainted.

Next minute, four burly policemen arrived on the front doorstep. They wanted to come in, too. I couldn't help but think that maybe I had overreacted a bit. I was shocked at seeing Kartya shooting up, but this was ridiculous. Apparently the neighbour heard all the screaming and called the police. The police thought it was a domestic dispute. They went into Kartya's room and found the syringe. They put it in a container and asked me if I wanted her charged with possession and use of a drug of dependence. I smiled and said, 'Why, so she can get another good behaviour bond?' The policeman looked at me and said, 'You've been through this before, have you?' I answered, 'Yeah, lots of befores. How come it needs four of you for a domestic dispute?' He laughed and told me that they were on their way to a burglary when they got the call; they were just passing our street. All my uninvited guests left. I took my hot rollers out, got dressed and went to work. As I drove, I hoped that Kartya would be all right. I wished I had handled the situation better. Me losing control didn't help Kartya. Her life was out of control already, and me reacting the way I did was only making it more difficult for her. She took off because she was ashamed of herself, because I had seen her feeding her addiction. Kartya rang me that night. Josh abused her for leaving me the way she did. She wanted to talk to me. She said, 'Mum, can I come home if I go to detox?' I said, 'Yes.'

Again, I got myself all churned up over the fact that she had to wait two weeks to get in. In the meantime, she continued to feed her addiction. She had to, she couldn't just stop. We knew that, so we all just continued on as usual. What else could we do?

Kartya and I went shopping to get all the things she needed to take with her, toiletries and some magazines. She packed her little bag and off she went to Dandenong. She asked me to keep looking for Lin-Ah-Hua. I promised I would. The kids wished her luck, told her to stay there and not go walkabout. She promised to stay and we believed she would. I thought that maybe this time it would work, but I wasn't getting my hopes up too high; we'd been down this road before.

Both Othmar and I knew that even if Kartya did detox, the same problems would still be there. They weren't going to go away. The only way she was going to be free was to heal on the inside. It was that pain that gave her the need for the drug in the first place. Without solving the main problem, we were simply going around and around in a circle. Kartya had to journey back to her past before she could journey into the future. She was always going to have an emotional illness. No matter how hard she tried—and at times she really struggled with her addiction— she couldn't begin to stay clean while her inner problem remained. Othmar and I could see that, so we owed it to her to do all we could to bring about a complete cure.

At times it was very painful to watch. She would create situations deliberately to give us the opportunity to turn our backs on her. She didn't want us to go through what we were all experiencing but, on the other hand, she was powerless to stop it. We needed her to realise that no matter what she did, even though we didn't like it and it hurt us all, we were not going to give up, not ever. We considered packing her up and taking her to Taiwan and searching for Lin-Ah-Hua, but we didn't know where to start. Financially we couldn't really do it. We could have mortgaged our house, but we didn't have one of those any more. That went long ago. We were now the proud renters of a little three-bedroom weatherboard, with six of us squashed inside. Maybe that's why we were all so close. We had no choice, we had to be nice to each other.

Pain

I'm not the reason for all your pain
Look at me, tell me, what's my name?
I'm not the birth mother
that left you alone
unwanted, unloved
with no name of your own
I didn't tie you down
and break your heart
deny you love and tear you apart
I picked you up to soothe your pain
imagined a future
with everything to gain
Loved and nurtured you
as if my own
Kept you safe and free from harm
then you took the needle
and put it in your arm
I'm not the reason for all your pain
Look at me, tell me, what's my name?

CHAPTER TWENTY-TWO

Light at the End of the Tunnel

It took me nearly two hours to drive to work every day. It was precious time on my own. I could think of things and no-one could get to me. It was 2 March 1998. I heard on the radio about a China Airlines crash in Taiwan. I pricked up my ears. It was being reported by an Australian journalist living in Taipei and his name was Ian Hyslop. I jotted his name down at the traffic lights and I made a mental note to try and find some way of getting his phone number. I would ring him. Surely, being a fellow Australian, he would help us track down Lin-Ah-Hua. No-one else had had any luck. I felt like time was running out. Kartya was still in detox. We were hoping she would stay there this time. If any of this was going to be of any lasting benefit, then we had to find her mother. When I got to work, I rang the radio station and they gave me Ian's phone number in Taipei. I was so excited. I had a gut feeling that this was going to lead somewhere. These days it didn't take a lot to get me excited. Getting up in the morning and finding that I still had a pulse and was breathing made me feel enthusiastic. Besides, I was still wearing my multicoloured jacket. It probably added colour to everyone else's life, too. A friend of mine told me that every time she looked at me she felt like putting her sunglasses on.

That night when I got home from work, I picked up the phone and made several attempts to dial the phone number in Taipei, but my hands kept shaking and I kept dialling the wrong number. I felt nervous and my hands were sweaty. I kept rubbing them together. I put my hand to my neck and I could feel my pulse thumping. I took a deep breath, picked up the phone and tried again. A lady with an Asian voice answered. I asked to speak to Ian Hyslop and she told me that he was out of town for a few days. She asked me if she could help. I thought she might have been a housekeeper, so I asked, 'What is your name?' She replied, 'I'm Kathy, Ian's wife.' I briefly told her Kartya's story and how much we wanted to find Lin-Ah-Hua. Her warm, reassuring voice put me at ease. She told me she had no doubt Ian would help us. He was unable to speak Chinese, said Kathy, but she was Taiwanese and could help with translations.

She asked me to send them all of Kartya's adoption papers and any other information we had. She said they would do their best. I got off the phone and went nuts. I felt like I'd hit the jackpot. I told the other kids and they were quite excited. Josh said, 'Good on you, Mum. You'll find her.' I loved the other three kids so much. They were very supportive, they always gave encouragement and were understanding. What this whole journey had taught them would be invaluable for their future understanding of other people, I believed. When I went to the detox unit that night to see

Kartya, I told her the good news. She was a bit blasé about it all. I can't say I blamed her; after all, we had been trying to find Lin-Ah-Hua for six years. Nevertheless, she did hope that this time we would be lucky and find her. I just hoped that her birth mother wanted to be found.

The thought had occurred to both me and Othmar that there was a possibility that either Lin-Ah-Hua didn't want to be found or, if we did find her, that maybe she didn't want to see her daughter. We decided to cross that bridge when we came to it. In the meantime, we had to be positive and pray for a successful outcome. I had always believed that her mother loved her and that she did not willingly give up her daughter. Kartya was a beautiful, healthy baby. A mother does not give up her baby for no reason.

I packaged up all Kartya's original adoption papers in both Chinese and English. I included an enlarged black and white photograph of Kartya, taken in the 'lawyer' Julie Chu's office. The photo showed the big, fat, healthy baby of about four months old. I also sent a story that Kartya had written on heroin, describing her battle with her addiction. I felt it only fair to Ian and Kathy to be honest about our situation. I wanted them to realise the urgency; the fact that if we didn't find Kartya's family and give her the answers that she so badly needed, then there was every possibility we would lose her. I also told him about the trial of Julie Chu. Even though we didn't know what had eventually happened to her, we did know that she had been jailed. We told Ian that we believed Kartya's adoption was legal and, to our knowledge, was never investigated. He would need all the information he could get if he was to find Lin-Ah-Hua.

A week after sending off the documentation, I got a fax from Ian and Kathy saying they were touched by Kartya's story. They said they would like to help and that with all the paperwork we'd provided it shouldn't be too difficult. When I showed the fax to Kartya, she was very excited. I think, for the first time, she really believed that someone was genuinely willing to help her. We were happy she could focus her mind on something positive. Now she began to feel good about herself. She was drug free and proud of herself for having lasted the eight days in detox. Our optimism was renewed when we saw a slow return of Kartya's self-esteem. Only two weeks after our initial contact with Ian, we got another fax.

Hi Nola and Kartya

Good news . . . Believe I've tracked down Mum . . . Have been to about half a dozen government agencies . . . and finally came up with an address . . . I've been there . . . and through Kathy have established that Lin-Ah-Hua lives there . . . however she was out when we visited . . . I'm waiting for a call and I expect to talk to her in the next few days. I will probably come to Melbourne and talk to you, how best to organise Kartya's meeting with her Mum.

I was at work when I got the fax. I burst into tears and started shaking my head. I felt sick in the stomach. I was walking around and around in circles. I thought, my God, I don't believe it. We have finally found her. This will save our daughter's life. I rang Othmar at work and told him. He was stunned. He couldn't believe it had happened so quickly. I couldn't wait to get home and tell Kartya. At least we now knew that Lin-Ah-Hua existed.

I had had a sneaking suspicion, which I had never shared with anyone, that maybe she was a fictional character; just a name to fill in the space on the adoption papers. But no, that was not the case, she really was out there.

I couldn't describe the feeling. I felt like I was on drugs. I drove all the way home with a big smile on my face, feeling euphoric. The traffic was heavy. A car had stopped next to me on the freeway. I was smiling away and the guy in the next car blew me a kiss. I felt like winding my window down and yelling out, 'Guess what? I've just found my daughter's mother.' I wanted to share our good news with the whole world. When I got home, I knew Kartya was there. The house had the distinct Chinese restaurant smell. She was in the kitchen cooking. I handed her the fax with a big smile on my face. She read it, then looked at me and said, 'Oh fuck, Mum. You're joking. I don't believe it, Mum. How can I believe it? This can't be true.'

I put my arms around her. She didn't tense up as usual. We hugged. Through tears I told her, 'You'd better believe it, Kartya, because it's true. We have found your mum.' Kartya spent all night ringing her friends, telling them that this Australian journalist had found her real mum. I didn't sleep at all that night. I kept having dreams that we'd found Kartya's mum. I woke up to find that it wasn't a dream.

The next few days were the happiest we had had in a long time. It was like a load had been lifted off our shoulders. For the first time in years, Kartya seemed to be at peace. We felt so happy for her. Now she would get the answer to her life's biggest question. Kiersten, Alex and Josh suggested we all go out for dinner to celebrate. They were so happy for Kartya. I think they thought that the dark cloud had been lifted and our life was going to get back to normal. I wondered if any of us would remember what a normal life was. After all, Josh was only fourteen when all this started. He was now twenty. It had been a long six years. However, if we could reunite Kartya with Lin-Ah-Hua and give her back her life, then it would all have been worthwhile. I wondered about the two older sisters on her adoption papers. I hoped Ian remembered to ask Lin-Ah-Hua about them.

I rang all our adoptive parent friends and told them the good news. They had lived through our pain and anguish over the years, especially my friend Pam. She was just as excited as me. She, of all people, knew how much this would mean to Kartya. I loved Pam. She has always thought that Kartya was wonderful. She never judged her by her addiction.

Othmar and I had wondered occasionally if anyone in Kartya's birth family had an addictive personality. So much about Kartya seemed to have a genetic link. By finding Lin-Ah-Hua, we would be able to find answers to a lot of questions.

Our elation was shortlived, however. Three days later we received another fax from Ian.

Hi Nola and Kartya . . .

Well, do you want the good news or the bad news first . . . First . . . Lin-Ah-Hua is not Kartya's mother . . . After finally pinning her down, she agreed to speak . . . She told me she served ten months in jail for 'lending her name' to the racket . . . She does not know who Kartya's birthmother is . . . The good news is . . . I've spoken to the Interior Ministry which controls the Police over here . . . outlined Kartya's story to a senior official and he's agreed to co-operate.

Secondly . . . A media company in Taipei are prepared to help organise a media campaign to track down Kartya's mother ...

I dropped the fax on the floor and froze. I couldn't believe this was happening. How could we tell Kartya? She would be crushed. None of this made any sense. For seventeen years we had believed Lin-Ah-Hua was Kartya's birth mother. If she was not her mother, then who was? Suddenly we had nothing, not even a name. Taiwan is an island with over twenty-two million people and we would be trying to find someone without a name. It was bloody hopeless, that's what I thought. What could we do? Tell Kartya to just forget about it all? Tell her we can't find her and that's that? Surely your birth mother can't be that important to you? Can't you just pretend that I'm your real mother? How simple that would be. But I knew that wouldn't happen.

I wanted to be able to find her birth mother for her. I would want someone to do it for me. If I was adopted, I would hope that my parents loved me enough to want to help me. I told Kiersten and Josh the news. They were shocked. They were worried about the effect on Kartya. When she came in, I showed her the fax. I let her read it herself. She got angry, very angry. She went into her room and turned her music up loud. I heard her crying. I knocked on the door and opened it. She told me to fuck off. An hour later, she'd gone. Packed her bags and left. I heard from her a week later. She was back on heroin.

I was worried that I'd never see Kartya again. As usual, I overreacted, got hysterical and started crying. Othmar tried to console me and said, 'Don't worry, she'll be back. Kartya's like a Velcro strip. She's stuck to us for good, no matter what she says.' That made me feel better. Velcro comes unstuck easily, but re-sticks constantly. A piece of Velcro can last a lifetime. I felt better. Othmar understood how I felt. Nobody else did. They didn't understand why I loved her so much. Our whole life was committed to our four kids. Just because Kartya was the one with problems didn't mean that we loved the others less. We just needed to help Kartya through her problems more than the others. That is the responsibility of any parent, but more so with an adoptive parent. Our children did not choose to be our children. They had no choice, we made the choice for them. How could we then walk away from them when they had problems? We knew when we adopted them that there was no guarantee of getting a perfect child. We also knew when we had our biological children that there were no guarantees attached to them. I know, because I looked and I didn't find one.

The blood running through the veins of Kiersten and Kartya may not have matched Othmar and me genetically, but it was the same colour: it was red. Whenever Kartya would go walkabout I would imagine what Othmar said about the Velcro strip and I would feel better. I would say to myself, 'You'll be back.'

It was never the same when she wasn't there. It was too peaceful and quiet. After so long with all the drama we had become used to it.

Othmar and I were not sure we were doing the right thing by pursuing the search. The chances were not all that good. Emotionally, we didn't think Kartya was up to it. She was deeply depressed. Were we just adding to her pain by taking her halfway around the world on a wild goose chase to try and find a nameless birth mother who possibly didn't want to be found? I was torn between thinking that we would find her and thinking, Nola, you are trying to achieve the impossible. Just when I felt like giving up, I got support from Kiersten, Alex and Josh. They told me I couldn't give up. They expected Othmar and me to keep trying. They believed it was possible. So I got renewed enthusiasm from them and continued with our original plan to land in Taipei and appeal to the people of Taiwan.

I had sleepless nights and nightmares about the whole situation but I told myself to just get her on that plane and deal with everything else then. Although if she didn't come home soon, we wouldn't be going anywhere.

The whole family's life was revolving around Kartya going to Taiwan and Kartya wasn't even around. If she stayed true to form, though, she would pop up some time in the next few days. If she was half as scared as I was, then the poor kid was terrified. At the end of the day, it was not going to be much consolation that I was still there for her. She wanted her 'real' mother, not the 'unreal' one who had been there all along. It's human nature that we all want what we think we can't have.

CHAPTER TWENTY-THREE
Best Laid Plans

~~~~

*G*an Hyslop arrived from Taiwan to outline the plans he had made to try and help us find Kartya's mother. When I first saw him, my first impression was of tallness. He put his arms around me and gave me a warm hug. I felt like I already knew him from our lengthy, expensive telephone calls. Othmar and I both sensed his genuine desire to help us. I trusted him immediately. He had a smooth radio announcer's voice that had a way of seducing you. With him was a journalist from *United Daily* newspaper in Taipei. His name was George Gao, a man in his early forties with a perpetual smile on his face and an infectious laugh. To our surprise, George told us that he was the journalist who had rung me at the restaurant, seventeen years before. He said that as soon as he had heard of our search, he wanted to be involved. He had covered the story of Julie Chu in 1982 and he wanted to finish the story he had started on our family all those years ago; the story that he couldn't run with because I wouldn't comment on anything at the time. Now George was here in Australia, helping us. We felt that it was a good omen. With George on our side, surely we would be successful.

Our whole family loved this gentle Taiwanese man who had great empathy with Kartya. He thought that hers was an amazing story and assured us that he would help as much as he could. He was going to run a story in the *United Daily* newspaper about a week prior to our intended arrival. Fortunately, Kartya returned home and George was able to interview her. We were proud of the fact that she was honest about her life and didn't at any stage hide her problems from him. After all, one of the main reasons she resorted to heroin, to take away the emptiness and dull the pain of not knowing who she was, was all part of the story.

George stayed in Melbourne for more than a week and interviewed the whole family. We trusted him to write an honest and sympathetic account and we believed that the publicity would give us more of a chance to reach the person we needed.

In the meantime, Ian had been organising footage of our family to be shown on Taiwanese television prior to our arrival. He introduced us to a cameraman named Steve Rossell. He would be filming the footage and would also be coming to Taiwan with us to film a documentary for Ian. We liked Steve, he had a casual, friendly approach to his work and Kartya felt very much at ease with him. We did some filming around the beautiful Royal Botanic Gardens and Southbank. It would show the Taiwanese people how lovely Melbourne was. When Ian and George left us to go back to Taiwan, they assured us that everything would be ready for our arrival in three weeks time.

I had written two letters to Taiwan: one to the Australian Commerce and Industry Office, outlining our intended visit and asking them for any help they could give us in our search for Kartya's mother; another I sent to the Criminal Investigation Bureau of Interpol in Taipei, also asking for help. I received a reply from the CIB's International Affairs Division almost immediately:

We have received your letter and learned that you will be travelling to Taiwan to look for your daughter Kartya's birth mother. We certainly will do our best to provide you with all necessary assistance.

Looking back on 1982, we understand it was such a big story that almost all the local media covered the story in detail. However, for some reason we are not able to obtain the original investigation file and photos. From the conviction record and your papers, the persons we may approach are Lin Ah-Hua (the registered legal representative of Kartya) and Julie Chu (the attorney). At this stage we have not yet located them.

To facilitate the identification, we will need a series of Kartya's photos since her childhood, especially the ones taken when she was adopted. As you will know, the local media is very enthusiastic and interested in your story. Please send us her photos as soon as possible.

When we received this letter from Interpol we felt a surge of hope. We were sure they would be able to uncover more information than we could about what had really happened back in 1982. We felt that with Interpol on our side we would get the facts sorted out. I sent them the photo of Kartya that was taken in Julie Chu's office, the one that showed her as a big, healthy, happy baby. That was the only one I sent because I thought any mother would recognise that face. I believed that photo showed how she was when she was last with her mother. Whatever happened after that, we couldn't begin to imagine. There was a lost five months from the time that photo was taken at four months, until she came in to our care at nine months. Of course we did have to consider that she might have been stolen from her mother. We just had to wait and see. We were not going to give up until we found out the truth.

I had a dream that the plane crashed, dropped out of the sky and fell into the ocean. It was the same stupid dream I had every time I had to fly. It put me on edge. I tried to push my fears to the back of my mind. I mentally locked them up and threw away the key.

Everyone was telling me that I was being very brave by taking Kartya back to find her birth mother and risking the chance that we could lose her. We didn't see it that way. Besides, we'd rather lose her to a birth mother than to heroin. At least we would still be able to see her. And anyway, the bravest thing I could do was get myself on that plane. Even though I'd flown many times, I continued to have the same dream. I began to think that if we got on that plane to Taiwan in two weeks, it would be a miracle.

Kartya wasn't at all relaxed. Tensions were high. She went walkabout again. Every time she felt pressure she took off, sometimes for days on end. Othmar and I were worried that she was not strong enough to cope with the pressure she was going to be under. Ian rang us from Taipei and wanted to know if we were ready and raring to go. I tried to sound positive and enthusiastic, but he sensed the strain in my voice. He knew how fragile the situation was. There was so much at stake. Everything had been organised. The accommodation had been booked—the Imperial Continental Hotel had generously sponsored us. Our airline tickets were donated by Cathay Pacific Airlines. The press conference had been arranged and the newspapers and other media informed of our impending arrival. All we needed was the guest of honour to go walkabout and not be there when the plane took off.

Kartya continued to float in and out of home and, two nights before we were to leave, we had a huge fight. Her behaviour was erratic; she was abusive, she screamed at me. I screamed at her. I told her that I didn't think she was ready to go, emotionally or physically. She screamed at me, 'Mum, I have to go. Can't you see that? If I'm not ready now then I'll never be ready.' She rang a friend, went out for the night and didn't come home. I lay awake, listening for her. I felt sick in the stomach, my heart was thumping out of my chest. Othmar was snoring away, oblivious to my insomnia. I was terrified that she was not going to reappear.

The day before we were due to leave, she turned up in her usual form as if nothing had happened and started packing her clothes. I breathed a sigh of relief and convinced myself that we were finally going. The thought of getting on the plane was starting to stress me. I tried not to show it. I got anxiety pains. I was not feeling too good. Kartya was showing signs of excitement about getting on a plane for the second time in her life. The first time was to come to Australia from Taiwan seventeen years before. Now she was going back. It was pretty scary for both of us. We didn't know what to expect. I was wishing that Othmar could come with us but someone had to earn money to pay the rent. We didn't even have much money to take with us—we were hoping someone would feed us over there.

We met Steve, our cameraman, at the airport. He was looking forward to the challenge. On the way to the plane we passed the airport bar. I wanted to nick in and have a few stiff shots of brandy, but I didn't. Eventually we were off, up in the clouds. My stomach was still somewhere back on the ground. I started to breathe more easily when we were above the clouds. Kartya was in good spirits.

She kept teasing me, saying, 'Mum, we're going to crash.' She was trying to make me look out of the window; she knew I never looked out of plane windows. I was relieved that we had finally made it. I had got her on the plane. Miracles do happen.

Kartya and I talked about what might happen when we got to Taiwan. I'd tried not to build her hopes up too high about finding her birth mother. I told her that just seeing her country of birth and meeting the people involved in her adoption would all be part of the healing process. She agreed with me. But deep in my heart I believed we would find her birth mother. I knew she would be out there somewhere. I didn't tell Kartya about the dream I had where I saw a beautiful young lady who at first glance didn't seem Asian but on looking closer was. There was something about her that was different, but I'm not sure what it was. I knew she existed and that I would know her when I saw her.

On and off I tried to sleep but without success. Every time I thought about arriving in Taipei I got the shakes. I was not sure if it was caused by apprehension or by the thought of spending ten days in one hotel room with Kartya. We couldn't spend five minutes in the one house without fighting; now we were going to spend ten days together under huge pressure. I knew I couldn't keep my mouth shut for ten days. I just prayed that a miracle would happen and we didn't have one fight. I didn't want her going walkabout in downtown Taipei. She had promised me that she would be a good girl, and I believed her. I always did.

I looked at Kartya, lying back in her seat, sleeping like a baby. When I looked at her face, I knew that we were doing the right thing. I knew this would help her figure out who she was. It would answer a lot of her questions. I didn't think she would have any problems assimilating into Taiwanese life. She would love the food. That would be one of her greatest joys: enough Chinese food to eat all day every day. The biggest problem would be the language. She wanted to learn to speak Chinese, so this trip might give her the incentive to learn her mother tongue.

When we finally arrived at Chiang Kai-shek Airport in Taipei, we were exhausted. We were starting to disembark when we heard our names over the loudspeaker on the plane. We wondered what had happened. Suddenly four airport security men arrived and ushered us through Immigration as if we were important people. They accompanied us to a main section of the airport where we saw a crowd gathered and cameras clicking away. There must have been about sixty cameras flashing. We were wondering who they were filming. We thought there must have been someone important arriving. Kartya jokingly said, 'Mum, maybe Michael Jackson's here.' Then all these cameras were coming at us, and they were all walking backwards, falling over each other, filming us. Then someone called out, 'Welcome back home, Kartya.' We were stunned. I had tears in my eyes. We arrived in Taiwan. It was 11.30 at night on Friday, 5 June 1998.

CHAPTER TWENTY-FOUR

Taiwan

The first thing that struck me when we walked out of the airport towards Ian's car was the warmth and humidity. It was very oppressive. I looked around and it seemed like the whole city was surrounded by hills. Somehow I always imagined it to be flat. I couldn't wait to see Taipei in daylight. Kartya's eyes were big as saucers. I was so proud of her. She may not have gone about things in the traditional way, in the way that most people follow their dreams, but she had screamed and kicked loudly enough for the world to hear her. If she hadn't gone about it in the way she did, we might not have heard her. We might not have realised the importance of her dream and she might have carried the pain around with her for the rest of her life— which probably wouldn't have been all that long, considering the lifestyle she was leading.

We piled our bags into Ian's car and off we went to our hotel, cameras following us in hot pursuit. Little did we know that this was a taste of things to come. We drove off through the streets. There were people everywhere, out shopping, eating in restaurants or just walking around with their children. I asked Ian, 'Don't they ever sleep here?' He said, 'No, not very often. Taipei is alive day and night.' I thought then that this would suit Kartya.

She loved the nightlife. As we dodged traffic and motorbikes through the streets, she sat in the back of the car and looked like a doll on a stick; her head was swivelling around in all directions as she tried to take in everything around us.

We were amazed by all the motorcyclists, hundreds of them at midnight, weaving in and out of the traffic often with two or three kids standing on the front. It all looked very hazardous to us Australians. We drove past the night markets, swarming with people, activity and colour. When we arrived at the Imperial Inter. Continental Hotel we had to go through a side door to avoid the cameras as they had arrived ahead of us. Kartya and I found it very curious that all of Taipei seemed interested in our little expedition. We went to our rooms and threw our bags down. The rooms were quite luxurious. I thought, I think I can handle ten days of this even if I do have to share with Kartya. Ian's wife, Kathy, told us that she was happy to be translating for us so we were glad to have her on board. Most Asian women I had met in the past were quiet and shy, but not Kathy. She was one of the strongest, most outgoing, enthusiastic women I have ever met. I always thought that I was a good talker until I met Kathy. She could talk and laugh all at the same time. We had a small snack together, then went to try and get some sleep, ready for the next day.

We sprawled out on our beds in our fancy room and I asked Kartya how she felt. She said, 'Mum, I feel great. This is my country.' I told her that I felt good too, and I was glad that we had come. We had a press conference organised for the Monday, so we had Saturday and Sunday free to look around Taipei. In the meantime, we needed sleep.

Neither of us slept very well. At 2 a.m., Kartya wanted to go out shopping. I told her to go back to sleep. Much to my surprise, she went back to sleep; for once, she did as I asked. I thought, things can only get better from here. The next morning, Ian, Kathy and their ten-year-old daughter Morgan came to the hotel to pick us up. Kartya and Morgan hit it off from the beginning. Morgan was fluent in English and Chinese. Being half Taiwanese and half Australian, she was a lovely-looking young lady. Steve, our cameraman, arrived and we went off to have a look at Taipei and to do some filming for our documentary. It wasn't easy because we had journalists, cameramen and photographers following our every move. They all wanted to get photos of the girl they called Kia. They followed us everywhere we went. Feeling like royalty, we moved surrounded by a huge contingent of media. With that sort of support and publicity, surely, we thought, we'll find this mother that we want.

The Taiwanese media were very supportive and gentle with us. We came to understand that without their help we had no chance of succeeding in our search. How could we possibly find someone when we didn't know who we were looking for? We knew nothing at all about Kartya's birth mother. We had no idea how old she was, what part of Taiwan she came from, nor if she had other family members who even knew about Kartya's birth. A friend of mine said, 'Nola, that's pie-in-the-sky stuff.' She offered to buy me a lotto ticket if we were successful. I was hoping that I would be able to take her up on her offer.

For the next two days we explored Taipei. Kartya's story had already been front page news for a few days, so when we went anywhere, people recognised the Chinese girl with the blonde-haired Australian mother. We walked the streets, went shopping, ate in the restaurants and everywhere people loved her and she loved them. I had never seen Kartya so happy.

Ian took us walking in the hills near Taipei. The whole city was surrounded by the greenest trees and mountains; it was an awesome sight standing high up on a mountain peak and looking down over Taipei. Kartya couldn't believe it. She thought Taipei was the most beautiful place in the world. She said to me, 'Mum, this is fucking wicked.' I threatened to wash her mouth out with soap if she didn't improve her vocabulary. She did promise me not to say the 'F' word in front of the media.

There were temples scattered throughout the hills where people went to pray every day. I thought to myself that this strange new culture and language Kartya seemed to be embracing with both arms open was her birthright. Steve was doing some filming of us on the top of the mountain, far away from anywhere, when this very old man with a walking stick came tottering up the hill. He stopped for a minute to see what we were doing, then he recognised Kartya. He said excitedly, 'Kia, Kia.' He smiled at us, nodded his head and kept on walking. It was amazing. Everyone knew her. She felt pretty special. It was so good for her self-esteem. It had taken a battering over the years and she was slowly starting to regain some self-respect.

Kartya interacted with Steve and Ian very well. She liked and trusted them both. Ian was her mentor on this journey and she listened when he spoke and looked to him for emotional support. They kidded around and joked together the whole time and Ian was able to get Kartya to do things that I would never have dreamed possible. In fact, Ian got me to do things that I would never have dreamed possible, like almost abseiling down a cliff edge with a hundred metre drop beneath me just to get a good shot for the documentary. When I kept reminding him that I was too old for all this, and that I didn't believe that I was allowing him to make me do it, he just said, 'Just think how good it'll look on film.' I said to him, 'Sure, I just hope that I live long enough to see it.'

Looking around this beautiful country, I couldn't help but wonder why more Australians didn't visit as a holiday destination. I'd never heard of anyone coming here for a visit, yet it was only eleven hours away and there was so much to see, as well as the warmest most friendly people you could ever wish to meet.

Taiwan is a long, thin island situated about one hundred and sixty kilometres off the eastern shore of mainland China. It is a mainly mountainous country and is only three hundred and ninety-five kilometres in length. The weather is subtropical with long hot summers and short mild winters. But with about twenty-two million people, on an island with just over half the square kilometres of Tasmania, it is one of the most densely populated countries in the world. One of their biggest celebrations is Chinese New Year which is on the first day of the lunar month in February. Everyone in Taiwan can be found out in their colourful best observing and participating in this special occasion which features ceremonial processions and dragon boat races and thousands of colourful lanterns. Taiwan is also a shoppers' paradise, with very modern air-conditioned tranquil department stores offering world-class shopping, as well as the teeming street markets that feature everything from watches, jewellery, shoes and clothes, to tiny little dogs in boxes.

Kartya's first attempt at shopping secured her three pairs of shoes, four tops and three skirts. Of course, she really needed them. When I said to her, 'Kartya, you don't have to buy everything on the first day,' she replied, 'But, Mum, I have to look good in case I find my mum.'

We were both getting a bit nervy about our press conference. Kartya went over and over her little speech. She had it all typed out on cue cards. I wondered how she was going to go; this girl who couldn't even talk to her family was going to get up in front of the whole of Taiwan and ask them to help her find her mother. It was putting a lot of pressure on her. She was still emotionally fragile. I believed that the tough streak in her would help her through the day. Besides, I would be there with her, supporting her. I knew she needed me to be there. She never actually said it, but somehow we had a relationship that stood the test of time. Even though we spent half our life fighting, we both knew that we loved each other unconditionally. I saw the best side of her when most people only saw the rebellious out-of-control teenager.

CHAPTER TWENTY-FIVE
Press Conference

Monday 8 June 1998 arrived. This was the day of the press conference when we were to appeal to the people of Taiwan to help us find Kartya's birth mother. We didn't know what to expect or how many people were going to be there, although Ian kept telling us that it would be big. At 2 p.m., hotel security staff came to our room and escorted Kartya and myself to the conference room inside the hotel. We walked in to a blaze of camera lights and flashing bulbs. I held Kartya's hand. We were both shaking. There was over one hundred people in the room, all representatives of the Taiwanese media.

We sat down at a long table laden with microphones. There was a huge bunch of flowers sitting in front of us. Also at the table were representatives from the Criminal Investigation Bureau, the Child Welfare League, the Taiwanese Government and Cathay Pacific Airways. Mr Christian Pirodon, the General Manager of

the Imperial Inter.Continental Hotel in Taipei, was there as was
Sam Gerovich from the Australian Commerce and Industry Office
and our wonderful new friend, Pauline Leung, from Compass
Public Relations Company, who organised the press conference.
Pauline and her staff, Sophie and Johnson, were helping with the
translations. Kartya kept looking at me. My eyes kept saying,
Don't worry, it's OK. We were overwhelmed by all the people with
cameras who were sitting right in front of us, photographing us
and filming our every move.

Ian strode confidently up to the microphone. He told the
media how he came to be involved in Kartya's story. He spoke
of his initial contact with us and how the story had unfolded. He
appealed to the media to help us.

Too quickly it was my turn. Nervously I approached the
microphone clutching my statement.

Good afternoon ladies and gentlemen of the press.

*I come to you today not as Kartya's birth mother, but as the
woman who for seventeen years has watched over her and
treated her as my own daughter. When my husband and I
adopted Kartya in 1981, we did not know that she was one of
many babies acquired illegally for the purpose of adoption.
The official documents we received named our new daughter
Lin-Mei-Li, the daughter of Lin-Ah-Hua. It was just months
ago that we found out that Lin-Ah-Hua served a jail term for
her part in the illegal baby-selling racket.*

*For six years we have tried to find Lin-Ah-Hua so we could
reunite her with Kartya, but with no success. Now that we
know she is not Kartya's birth mother, our search starts all
over again. Why is it so important for us to find her?*

Well, we have watched Kartya's identity crisis for many years. Ever since she was a small girl she has asked me the same questions many times. Who is my birth mother? Why was I given away? These are the questions that have caused her distress and many emotional problems.

It is my duty to help her find her birth mother. I love my adopted daughter. I owe it to her to help. Kartya was born around July 1980. We believe she was born in the Chung-Ho area. I know Kartya is not the only victim of this baby-selling racket. I know there are mothers out there who gave their babies up or were forced to give them up. Please come forward and talk to us. Your help will give peace of mind to the adopted daughter I love. Thank you for your help.

I went back to my seat and sat down. I was shaking like a leaf. I looked at Kartya. She got up, threw her head and shoulders back and walked up to the lectern. She looked strong and confident. I was so nervous for her, I grabbed hold of Sam Gerovich's hand. Kartya commenced.

Good afternoon ladies and gentlemen of the press and assembled guests . . .

Today, I would like to thank you for coming to hear my plea for help. I left Taiwan seventeen years ago as a small baby, too small to know who I was, too small to know who my parents were. The name on my adoption papers was Lin-Mei-Li. I became Kartya Wunderle, living in a land far from my birth country.

As I grew up in Australia, I found out I was one of more than sixty babies adopted to parents overseas illegally.

I don't know if I was stolen or sold, and the thought of having a family out there somewhere in Taipei has caused me much pain and concern over the years.

I want very much to meet my biological mother, to ask her why I was adopted, to see if I have any brothers and sisters . . . If I was stolen, my mother must surely have prayed for my future. If she was unwed and gave me up, she must wonder what happened to me. If my mother was poor and sold me, she must often think of the little baby girl she was forced to cast out of her house. I come to Taiwan, with only love in my heart for a mother who did what she did because she had to. I love my Australian parents, but it is important for me to find out the Big Mystery in my life . . . **Who is my mother?** *I hope you can help me.*

Kartya strode back to her seat with tears streaming down her face. I grabbed her hand. She looked at me with tear-filled eyes. I was so proud of her. There was not a dry eye in the room, Kartya's passionate plea for help had touched everyone. After more speeches from the assembled guests, and lots more photos and questions, we were escorted back to our room. All we could do now was hope that Kartya's mother saw and recognised her, and was able to come forward.

We had already been advised by Interpol that mothers were coming forward in the hope that Kartya was their daughter. We went to their headquarters to meet with their officials. A short, efficient, businesslike man with glasses, Ke Ching-Chung, was assigned to take charge of the investigation. We called him Mr Kay. Dressed in a pristine white shirt and blue tie, he greeted us with a warm, firm handshake. He told us that he had been working diligently on Kartya's case for several months. I asked him if he thought that Kartya might have been stolen from her mother. He said he did not think so. The best way to find Kartya's mother, he felt, was through the media, and if Kartya's mother wanted to come forward, she would. I asked him what he thought our chances were. He said, 'Good, very good.' He looked at Kartya and said, 'Don't worry, we will find your birth mother, I am sure.' Kartya was very happy with that. As we left, I thanked Mr Kay for helping us. He told us that he had great empathy for the story of Kartya because he had a little girl himself. I shook his hand and as we left I thought to myself what a lovely person he was. He also had a nice smile.

We found all the people in Taiwan to be like that, genuinely warm and friendly. When we got back to our hotel, the papers were full of Kartya's story. Over sixty daily newspapers carried news on the Australian girl's search. Every television station covered the press conference. With that sort of coverage, we felt sure something would happen. Kartya was feeling very positive. She said to me, 'Mum, if my mother's still in Taiwan, I'm sure she knows it's me.'

I'd never thought about the fact that her mother might not have even been in Taiwan any more. People do move about and, after all, it was seventeen years ago. Anything could have happened. Her mother might not have been alive. I was not prepared to entertain any of those thoughts. If I began to think like that there would have been no point in staying. I rang Othmar at home every day to let everyone know what was happening. Already there was news of Kartya in the Australian newspapers and on television. Josh was busy taping everything for us. They missed us very much and were hoping that we were successful. They were all pretty proud of their sister for having the courage to try. Nobody understood Kartya more than those kids and, despite everything that had happened in the past, they still loved her.

In Taiwan I tried to spend a bit of time each day alone with Kartya going over what was happening. I thought this would help to lessen the burden. She seemed to be handling things very well, especially the media. She appeared on several television talk shows and was very relaxed and calm as she appealed for her mother to come forward.

Ian and Kathy were with us most of the time. Kathy was flat out translating every word so that we didn't miss anything. There was no way we could have done any of this without their help. We would always be grateful, even if we didn't find Kartya's mother.

The whole experience was invaluable for Kartya. We had been here nearly five days and she hadn't had a mood swing. This was highly unusual. Kartya was the queen of mood swings. One every day was normal. I was keeping my fingers crossed.

I lay on my luxurious bed, in our luxurious room, in our luxurious hotel wondering how on earth I had arrived where I was. Me, the girl from Geelong, one of ten kids, with a passion for Candy Pink lipstick, who married the tall, dark, handsome man with the foreign accent. I had four kids and loved them with a passion— but I couldn't use the video recorder, didn't know my left from my right, couldn't use a computer, couldn't swim, and had an abnormal fear of flying. Yet here I was dragged halfway around the world by a ratbag daughter to find a birth mother without a name. I couldn't help but wonder where this journey would lead. But I wasn't getting off. I was staying on this bus to its final destination because this was the trip of a lifetime.

I looked at this daughter of ours, sleeping soundly in her luxurious bed and looking every bit like the archangel Gabriel and I told her: You are what this is all about. To make you happy. That's all we ever wanted. To see you free of the big gorilla clinging to your back, weighing you down.

I woke the angel because today Kartya had to go for the blood test at the CIB headquarters. We arrived with Ian, Kathy and Steve. Mr Kay met us at the door—so did the media of Taiwan. They all wanted a photo of the Australian girl having a blood test. We got into the lift with cameras and journalists all crammed in. We couldn't breathe. We met with the chiefs of the CIB and they outlined the procedure. We were all squashed in this little room with camera lights popping. The heat was unbelievable. Mr Kay told us that some of the mothers who had come forward had already had the blood test. Results would still be a week or so away. We were surprised because we hadn't been confident anyone would come forward. There were all these mothers out there in Taipei who had lost babies seventeen years ago. It was astounding.

My mind recalled one of the letters we received several months before coming to Taiwan. It was from an official agency we had contacted for help to find Kartya's mother. It said that when a Chinese mother gives up her baby, she turns her back on the child forever. I never believed that; I told Kartya that I didn't believe her mother had turned her back on her. It was my gut instinct. Now our feelings were being proven right.

We left the CIB feeling very hopeful. Kartya wanted to go to a Buddhist temple and pray so Ian and Kathy took us to Tsu Huei Temple in Sungshan, one of the ten great temples in Taipei. It is a huge and majestic bright red temple with people flowing in and out of gigantic doors and is situated at the foot of Fushou mountain, part of a lush green mountain range. As we walked in to the temple, a feeling of peace and tranquillity filled my body. Kartya grabbed my arm. Her eyes were like saucers as we walked through the great hall. Offerings of fruit were spread out over the altar. There were women dressed in blue gowns everywhere. They wrapped a gown around each of us and tied it with a sash and then presented us with incense sticks to light and hold. Then they showed us how to pray, kneeling in front of the altar with our hands clasped around the incense sticks and our heads bowed. We prayed for Kartya's mother to have the courage to come forward. Everyone at the temple prayed with us and for us. They all knew Kartya's story and offered such encouragement that we felt this miracle we wanted so badly would happen. All we had to do was be patient.

I was starting to feel a bit tired; I missed Othmar and the kids. I was worrying about them too—not that I needed to, they were quite capable of looking after themselves. I just didn't want to return without a resolution. I didn't want to go back to our life the way it was. I wanted to go back feeling that we had completed the circle, that we had helped Kartya to find out who she was. For her to be able to look in the mirror and see herself.

CHAPTER TWENTY-SIX
Links in the Chain

There are two key players in Kartya's story and we wanted to meet them both. One was Lin-Ah-Hua, the birth mother named on Kartya's adoption papers. The other was Julie Chu, the law clerk who arranged the adoption. Ian had organised for us to meet with them separately. We set off first to meet Lin-Ah-Hua. Ian, Kathy, Steve, Kartya and I all piled into the car and drove from one end of Taipei to the other. We travelled up laneways and through villages until we finally came to a freestanding building in a not-so-affluent part of town. Steven Chang, one of the journalists from the *United Daily*, was already there. Wherever we went, Steven came. He needed any news he could find to print in 'Kartya's Diary' section of the daily paper. He would inform the people of Taiwan what was happening with Kartya's search for her mother. He wrote about where we had been and who we had seen in relation to our search. We loved Steven, he was always welcome to be with us.

A lady was standing at the front door. She looked about fifty years old and wore white pedal pushers and a purple sequined top. Her hair was short and curly. I felt very strange. Kartya looked on edge. Kathy introduced us to Lin-Ah-Hua. We shook hands. She had tears in her eyes. We went upstairs to a sort of kitchen-cum-sitting room. It was very hot and humid. Lin-Ah-Hua kept looking at us. She looked worried. She probably thought we were angry with her, but we just wanted her to tell us what she knew. Kartya said to her, 'Do you know what you have done to me? All my life I thought you were my mother and you're not.' Lin-Ah-Hua answered, 'I am sorry. I did not know what I was doing. I spent ten months in jail away from my family for what I did.'

She told us her story. How she had been very poor, with a family to feed. She was working at the market one day when a lady approached her and asked her if she could have her Household Registration papers for a day. This document is a government requirement for all inhabitants of Taiwan. It lists each family member's name, address and identification number. When a new baby is born it is added to the registration papers. The lady told Lin-Ah-Hua that she would pay her. Lin-Ah-Hua needed the money. She gave the lady her papers. It wasn't until she was arrested by the police that she found out what the papers had been used for: to put her family details on Kartya's adoption papers. Lin-Ah-Hua said, with tears in her eyes, 'If I had known what I was doing, I would never have done it.' Kartya was crying. She said, 'Do you know who my mother is?' Lin-Ah-Hua said, 'I am sorry, but I don't know. I know I am not your mother. I wish I was. You are a beautiful girl. I would be honoured to be your mother.' She told Kartya that if she didn't find her birth mother, then she would like to be her surrogate mother in Taiwan. She would be welcome to come and stay with her whenever she liked.

We hugged Lin-Ah-Hua. I said, 'Maybe you could be Kartya's Taiwanese adoptive mother?' She replied, 'Oh no, I could never be that. I am not qualified. That would take a very special mother.' She was so simple, so sweet and humble. I could see that not only was Kartya a victim in this whole story but so was Lin-Ah-Hua.

From this meeting Kartya did get answers to questions that had played on her mind for years. One barrier had been removed. We left feeling sad that Lin-Ah-Hua couldn't offer us any more help, but better for having met her. We made a promise to meet her again one day. She said if that did happen, it would be an honour for her. She hugged us both as we left and she wished Kartya luck in finding her mother. She said she would pray for her.

I could tell it had been emotionally draining for Kartya. After looking at her adoption papers for so many years, memorising them, she had become Lin-Mei-Li, daughter of Lin-Ah-Hua. That was imbedded in her mind. She would have been better off to have nothing because, in the end, that's all she had, nothing. The pain of losing what she thought she had was worse than not having it to start with.

The Chinese appear to place a very high value on family life. No matter where we went in Taipei, we would see families together— parents with young children, teenagers and grandparents all happily interacting. They would shop together at the night markets and travel together in groups to the temples to pray. Whenever we went to restaurants, we were always surrounded by families eating together with the grandparents nursing the baby of the family. The family unit seemed very close and tightly knit. I wanted so much to be able to find a family like that for Kartya: a big extended family.

I felt proud that despite our turbulent six years, we had still managed to maintain a closeness within our family, a bond that was, perhaps, strengthened by the pressures we found ourselves under. I was grateful that it hadn't gone the other way and torn us apart. This was such a huge step for us all to take, it wasn't just for Kartya, it was for Kiersten, Alex and Josh; this trip to Taiwan involved the whole family. It was important that we tried to put all the bits of the puzzle together. We had to try and find all the people involved so that in the event that we didn't find her birth mother, at least she would feel that something had been achieved, and so would we.

I felt that we had all been blessed by a guardian angel. The number of people in Taipei who were helping us was inspiring and astonishing. We knew we could not have achieved as much as we had without their support.

Kartya very much wanted to meet Julie Chu. She needed to hear Julie tell her personally everything she knew about the first eight months of her life. Ian and Kathy organised a meeting at their house. Kartya and I were both feeling very nervous. So many questions were going around in my mind. I didn't know what to feel about Julie Chu. Maybe, in the end, it would turn out that she was a victim, as well? I knew, though, that Kartya felt angry with her.

When Julie walked in with her lawyer and sat down, our eyes met. She was smaller than I had imagined. Almost fragile. I looked at her face; she was pretty. She had sad eyes and they were full of pain. Instinctively I put my arms around her and we both cried. I cried because if it wasn't for her we would not have had Kartya. Even though it had been rough, very rough, we were still glad that she was our daughter. There was never a question of that. I immediately felt that we had all walked a painful road, but in different directions. I realised then that we had forgiven her. She was just another person involved in this sad situation. Many people had played their part. We couldn't blame her entirely.

Kartya was crying and her anger was being washed away with her tears. She asked lots of questions. Julie told us that she had broken the law. She had used incorrect details on the adoption papers. She had served six years in jail. She told us that she herself was adopted and she had wanted to help babies to find loving homes. That, she said, was the reason she had done it.

Kartya was surprised when Julie said that she, too, had been adopted. It seemed to put a different perspective on things. Julie told us that without the forged adoption papers, the babies could not go to a new home. I asked her if she had any idea why Kartya had been so badly neglected, both physically and emotionally. Why had she been tied by the wrists and ankles? Julie said that because she had paid other people to look after the babies, she was unaware of the level of care that they had received. She told us that, to her knowledge, Kartya had been cared for by several different families over the five-month period it took for the adoption to be finalised.

It suddenly clicked in my mind. Several different families! How many? Two, four, maybe more? I was now beginning to understand the terminology, 'Failure to thrive due to emotional deprivation.' Kartya had missed out on the one-to-one love and care so necessary for a small baby. That was when she started to build the brick wall around her emotions. It went right back to the first nine months. She had not been able to identify anyone as her primary caregiver. There had been no one person she could trust to fulfil her needs so she had shut down emotionally. I thought of the care that Othmar and I had given to Kiersten, Alex and Josh: twenty-four-hour love and devotion, fulfilling their every need, being there all the time. Deprived of this basic care for so long, how could she begin to trust us? It was all making sense.

Julie told us that most of her adoption records had been destroyed. She had no idea who Kartya's birth mother was because most of the babies came through a middle person. She said it was possible the middle person might have more details as to where Kartya came from. Julie said that she would try and contact this person and we could meet her. Kartya was very despondent. All hope of Julie having anything fruitful to give us was gone.

Julie told Kartya that she was sorry if we blamed her. 'I thought I was doing a good deed, but I only have to look at you to know that what I did was right. You are a beautiful girl with a beautiful family,' she said. I think deep down, Kartya agreed with her. Kartya said that she did forgive her and asked her if she would help to find her real mother. Julie said she would. We parted, sadly, but still with hope. Julie handed us a statement that she was going to give to the media:

It is out of the basic desire of human nature, and out of the natural emotional link between family members, that Kartya, the young girl, has travelled a long way across the ocean to Taiwan in search of her kin. Her determination and courage is indeed touching and admirable. However without the complete knowledge of the entire facts regarding this event, some of the media should have used the title 'A Case of Baby Trading' to throw a dark shadow on Kartya's journey to search for her relatives, which has caused a distortion of the fact that this event was by nature a practice of good feelings. More than ten years ago, I was engaged in Social Services work, and was entrusted, on behalf of children whose biological mothers did not apply for residential registrations, to handle the procedures of adoption by appropriate overseas individuals. Since the girl's biological guardian refused to leave any personal particulars, and since I was not familiar with the law, I handled this case by having this baby registered as being born to some other person, thus breaking the law, by mistake. Nevertheless, at that time a consent/agreement was signed by all involved, so how could the allegation of 'baby trading' be justified? Morever, after the extensive coverage of this event by the media, a number of mothers have appeared and offered to have their DNA examined and compared to Kartya's, yet none of them has ever heard that any 'baby trading' or 'baby stealing' was involved during that period. It is obvious that the facts and truth do not fit into some of the media's reports about the so-called 'baby trading'. It is my request that the media give unbiased coverage to make absolutely sure that they will not cause damage to the country, the society and to myself. I have reiterated many times, that it is a beautiful action of passion and kinship that Kartya crossed the ocean looking for her relatives, and I will do all I can to help her. However, I can't expect to be of much help, because of incomplete documents that are still available after seventeen years, and also, at the time I was only acting as agent on behalf of overseas adoptive parents to have such procedures as notarial certificates, etc, done in Taiwan. It is my hope that, through the concerted efforts of the media and the people of Taiwan, the girl, Kartya, will succeed in finding her mother, so that my own desire can also be satisfied. Julie Chu

The next day, Julie and her husband Tony, a warm and generous man who was typical of the Taiwanese we had met, Ian and Kathy, Kartya and myself, drove to an outer suburb of Taipei to meet with Mrs Zehn, the middle person in the adoption triangle. She had also served time in prison for her part in the adoptions. She was a tall, thin lady, about forty years old. She lived with her husband in a small, poky flat, in a long, narrow laneway. She told us that when she was given a child, by either an unmarried mother or a poor family, and they were unable to care for the child, she always got an agreement signed by the mother, declaring that the child was given up willingly and that the birth mother agreed to the adoption of her baby.

She proceeded to pull out a big box stuffed full of agreements. Kartya was hopeful that inside the box were papers relating to her. I wasn't very optimistic. After all, we had no name, no details whatsoever. We didn't know who we were looking for. I pulled out the baby photo taken in Julie Chu's office, showing a big fat healthy baby and asked Mrs Zehn, 'Do you remember Kartya?' Mrs Zehn said, 'Yes, I do remember her. She was very dirty and sick when she came to me.'

Kartya's eyes lit up and she asked, 'Do you remember who brought me to you?' After much thought, Mrs Zehn replied, 'I think it was a young schoolgirl, but I don't remember. It was such a long time ago.' I wondered how she remembered the condition of Kartya when she couldn't remember who had brought her in for adoption. Judging by the number of agreements in the box, I doubted the clarity of her memory. I didn't think she had much to offer us and I didn't really believe her. Kartya had been well cared for in her first four months, you could see that from her photo. I wasn't prepared to believe that a mother gave up a healthy beautiful baby, not after caring for her for four months. Mrs Zehn, I believe, genuinely wanted to help, but time had confused her memory. We were not going to discover Kartya's birth mother from her. As we left, we thanked her and she wished us luck in our search. She pulled Kartya aside and said, 'I'm sorry for what has happened to you, but it was not my fault. I was doing a good deed. I hope you believe me.' Kartya nodded and walked away with tears in her eyes. As we drove off, I turned and waved. Mrs Zehn was wiping tears from her eyes.

Julie and Tony promised to continue to help us in our search.

That night we went to a restaurant with Julie and Tony. We had our own private room. As we consumed the most wonderful Chinese food, they told us of the events that had led them both to be imprisoned. It had been a difficult time for them. They had been separated from their family and ostracised by the community. They still believed that what they had done was in the best interests of the children. I was not going to disagree with that. If we had not been able to adopt Kartya, I did not want to think what could have happened to her.

When we got back to our hotel room, I could tell that Kartya was depressed. I explained to her that we had every reason to remain optimistic; after all, we had no results of the DNA tests. Many mothers had come forward and were requesting blood tests. We had been in Taiwan a week, but it seemed a lot longer and we were both feeling the pressure. The CIB were keeping very quiet about the test results so far. I assumed they only wanted to tell us positive news. In the meantime we played the waiting game and continued to explore the beautiful town of Taipei. It was, though, hard to get completely into holiday mode with so much at stake.

CHAPTER TWENTY-SEVEN
Penghu

We were invited by a local politician to fly down to the island of Penghu. It is situated in the middle of the Taiwan Strait and the Penghu Archipelago, which consists of sixty-four islands of varying sizes. It would be two days away from the 'looking for birth mother' pressure.

We boarded a small plane. It had only about twenty seats and I'd never heard the name of the airline. I don't like big planes, but little ones I like even less. This would, however, be a nice break away from the media and I couldn't back out. Kartya was looking forward to it. Ian and Kathy were with us. They sat back and read the newspapers. Kartya looked out the window. I sat terrified, sweaty hands gripped the seat. God, I wished I didn't feel like this. Why couldn't I look out the window? Why couldn't I even pretend to read the papers? Every time the plane as much as shook I thought, that's it, we're going to finish up in the South China

Sea. We didn't. We all arrived in one piece—but all I could think of was that I would have to get back on that small plane to return to Taipei.

As we walked off the plane, I could tell it was a beautiful island. The sky was so blue, the air was so clear and fresh. We were met by the politician, Mr Leonard Hsu from the Democratic Progressive Party. He was a charming man with steel grey hair who spoke fluent English—and who had the media with him. So much for our break away from the media. Next we were filmed walking up and down the streets hand in hand with the politician. I decided not to let this little political exercise ruin my trip.

Kartya was getting edgy. I said to her, 'Hang in there. We go to lunch in a minute.' We were escorted into a little restaurant. Upstairs we went into a small room all set up for lunch: lunch with about thirty media personnel and cameras. Kartya looked at me and whispered in my ear, 'What the fuck are they all doing here?' I said to her, 'Well, I guess we have to do it if it helps to find your mum.' She calmed down and we enjoyed the local cuisine for lunch amid the assembled members of the press. They asked Kartya lots of questions as she ate. Ian was trying to coach her through them, but it all got too much. She burst into tears and walked out of the room. It was so hot, the room was like an oven. I wasn't surprised that it had all overpowered her.

After a while she returned, sat down and resumed eating as if nothing had happened. Everyone was very understanding and I think they realised the pressure was becoming a bit too much.

After lunch, Mr and Mrs Wang-Lin, a wonderful couple who lived on the island, drove us everywhere. It was heaven. Houses were dotted everywhere throughout green rolling hills that stretched the length and breadth of the island, mostly two-storey houses with lots of glass and painted with a white wash. Penghu was surrounded by ocean. They took us out in a glass-bottom boat, over the aqua blue water to look at the magnificent coloured coral. Later, we took a speedboat to one of the smaller islands in the group. It was merely a dot on the map. Kartya went for a swim in the clear sparkling sea. As we walked on the golden sand down to the gently lapping waves, we saw four old men sitting on the edge of the water under a little wooden hut. We momentarily stopped and looked at them. Immediately they started pointing to Kartya, saying, 'Kia, Kia.' We were on a little island in the middle of the South China Sea and some old men on the beach knew the story of Kartya. It amazed us.

The inhabitants of these islands live a very simple life. There is no rush to get anywhere. They all have an air of peace and tranquillity about them. Kartya and Ian went for a ride on a small motorbike. Kartya sat on the back as Ian raced around the island. This tall lanky Aussie was a bit of a kid himself at times. We stayed in a lovely hotel and Kartya and I had our own rooms. Kartya was thrilled that she got to spend one night without me— although neither of us got much sleep. Mr and Mrs Wang-Lin, the couple who were showing us around the island, had made so many plans for us that we were still visiting people at two o'clock in the morning.

When I finally got to bed and went to sleep, I had the most vivid dream. It was just like the one I had at home of the beautiful Asian lady who somehow looked different. This time she came and put her arms around me. It was so clear. I believed with all my heart that it was Kartya's mother and that she would come to us. The next morning, Kartya was feeling very despondent. She was tired and the pressure was getting to her. She said to me, 'Mum, I want to go home. I want to give up this fucking dream. We're never going to find her. The whole idea was stupid to start with.'

I said, 'Kartya, look at me. Look into my eyes. We will find your mother. We are not leaving Taiwan until we do. I promise you, we will find her. Do you believe me?' Her eyes filled with tears and she said, 'Yes, Mum, I believe you.'

We all got back on the little plane. I gripped the seat with sweaty hands, imagining, once again, that we were going to fall into the South China Sea. When we arrived at Taipei we went straight to our luxurious hotel room and sprawled out on our beds, exhausted after two of the most wonderful days we had ever had. The phone rang. It was Mr Kay from Interpol. He said, 'Mrs Wunderle, please don't leave Taiwan yet.' My heart started pounding. I knew that a lot of mothers had been for the DNA tests and so far we hadn't heard any results. I asked if he had any news for us and he replied, 'No, not yet. Let's just say that I have a smile on my face.' I wondered what he meant and prodded him. 'Mr Kay, have you found her?' He said, 'I cannot confirm anything until tomorrow. Just don't leave Taiwan. And don't tell anyone about my phone call.' Shaking, I hung up the phone. I was overwhelmed with the thought that *she* had been found. I didn't tell Kartya. I didn't want to tell her something that I didn't know for sure myself. We would wait until tomorrow. But I couldn't sleep in anticipation of what the next day might bring.

The next day we went shopping to the Sogo department store in Taipei. We had cameras following us, so it was a bit hard to shop. The media all wanted something to put on their evening news. We were understanding of that. Everyone in Taipei knew the story of Kartya. They all wanted to know if she'd found her mum. Everyone was very sympathetic and understood her need to know her family. We were grateful for the enormous support that everyone in Taiwan had shown us.

Kathy bought me a bottle of Femme Parfume by Marcel Rochas. It was my favourite and I hadn't been able to get it in Australia for years. It had nostalgic memories for me: it was the first perfume Othmar had bought for me, nearly thirty years ago. When I sprayed some on, I instantly felt thirty years younger. When I told Kartya, she answered in typical teenager fashion, 'Mum, I hate to tell you, but you don't look thirty years younger.' I knew I didn't, she didn't have to tell me. When this was all over, I looked forward to going back home and sleeping for a week. I just hoped I didn't wake up to find it had all been a dream.

When we got back to the hotel and Mr Kay rang, I knew. He said in a gentle, professional voice, 'Mrs Wunderle, I'm pleased to inform you that from a DNA test completed today, we are very happy to confirm that Kartya's birth mother has been found. I am currently making arrangements for Kartya to meet her mother.' I screamed, 'Oh my God. Oh, God. Kartya, your mother's been found. We've found your mother . . . Mr Kay, thank you, thank you so much. I love you,' I shouted down the phone.

Kartya started crying, 'Mum, I don't believe it. Are you sure? I don't believe it. Oh, fuck, are you sure?' We couldn't stop crying. I was thinking, God, now we have found her, what if she wants to keep her? What if she wants her to live here? Oh well, we would just have to deal with that when the time came. I knew, though, that the main thing was we had achieved a bloody miracle. Many people had said we didn't have a chance, that we were looking for a needle in a haystack. But we had found one mother in a land of twenty-two million people—and we didn't even know her name. Yes, I thought, miracles do happen. Anything is possible. This was worth everything, it was even worth all the pain we went through. To see Kartya so happy, so absolutely stunned to think that she was going to meet her mother after all these years was worth any price. I even knew what she looked like, because I had seen her in my dream.

I was so excited you would have thought it was my mother we had found. My first thoughts were with Othmar. He was waiting at home. I had to tell him. We were in this together, him and me, right from the very beginning. We had stuck together for thirty years and when things got bad we had never given up. We took each day one at a time. We even hung on to each other when we had nothing else to hang on to. I would say to him sometimes, 'Othmar, when the going gets tough, the tough get going.' He'd say, 'Sure, but does it have to get this tough?' When we had to deal with Kartya's addiction—something that we didn't really want to deal with and didn't really know how to deal with—the only thing we were sure of was that we were not going to give up. We both knew that; we didn't even have to discuss it. Somehow it gave us both strength knowing that neither of us was prepared to walk away from it. We both loved Kartya. Giving up was never an option. It was always a matter of, 'OK, what do we do next? How do we handle this?'

I was shaking as I picked up the phone to dial our number at home in Australia. Josh answered. I said, 'Josh, we've found Kartya's mum. Get Dad.' I heard him call out to Othmar. His voice was urgent. 'Dad, quick, it's Mum. They've found Kartya's mum.' Othmar answered, 'Hello.' I couldn't speak. No words would come out of my mouth. The lump in my throat prevented me from saying a word. He said, 'Are you there? Are you all right?' I burst into tears. Finally I said, 'Othmar, we've got a match.' He said, 'Oh, thank God, thank God for that.' We were both crying, we couldn't say anything else. We were hysterical with happiness. We both knew that this would save Kartya's life. I told him to get on the next available plane and come. We needed him to be here. He said he would. When I hung up, we were both still crying.

I knew Kiersten, Alex and Josh would feel the same. After all, they were the ones who had given me the encouragement to keep trying. They knew that this was something that Kartya had to do; that she would never be at peace if she didn't go on this journey. They respected her and never at any stage did they question her decision to try and find her mother. Kiersten once said to me, 'Mum, only when she finds her real mother, will she realise that you are her real mother.' Suddenly, though, it seemed as if none of that mattered any more. All that mattered was that we were able to reunite Kartya with the family that she had dreamt about all her life.

CHAPTER TWENTY-EIGHT

Success, at Last

M r Kay from Interpol rang in the afternoon and arranged to pick us up from the hotel in the evening. He said that he wanted to take us out for coffee. I knew there was more to this than just coffee, but I didn't say anything to Kartya. She was still overwhelmed by the fact that her mother had been found and was both excited and apprehensive about meeting her. She said to me, 'Mum, what if she doesn't like me?' I told her, 'Kartya, there is no chance of that. Your mother has come forward because she loves you. She's probably thinking the same as you. Trust me, she will like you.'

When Mr Kay arrived, I hugged him and thanked him for all his work. He said, 'You don't need to thank me. I was only doing my job.' He explained that he was still trying to arrange a meeting. In the meantime, he said, we would go out for coffee to discuss certain aspects of the case. Ian and Steve, our cameraman, were in our room when Mr Kay arrived. I don't think they believed that we were just going for coffee. They wanted to be with us when we met Kartya's family. We could understand that; after all, they had been there from the very beginning. Mr Kay was very matter of fact and said, 'OK, let's go.' We left, leaving Ian and Steve wondering where he was taking us.

It was eight o'clock at night. We hopped into his car and drove around the streets of Taipei. He asked Kartya several times if she thought that she was a stolen baby. She said she didn't know. All she wanted was the truth about what had happened seventeen years ago. He told her that she had not been stolen. He told us no details about her mother or her family. After driving up laneways and down roads for about half an hour, Mr Kay pulled his car into a side street and stopped. He turned around and said, 'Kartya, are you ready? You're going to meet your mother now.'

Kartya looked at me. She looked scared. I felt like I was going to be sick. After all the pressure of the last two weeks, I still couldn't believe that I was actually going to meet my daughter's birth mother. I kept taking deep breaths to try and take away the nervousness I was feeling. Mr Kay read to us a press statement that he said would be released to the media and people of Taiwan.

THE THIRD PRESS RELEASE BY THE CRIMINAL POLICE BUREAU *in regard to helping Australian girl Kartya to come to Taiwan in search of her biological mother.*

After more than three months' investigation, comparisons of DNA *and interviewing those who are involved, today, the 16th June 1998, the* CRIMINAL POLICE BUREAU *confirmed that Kartya's biological mother has been found. In accordance with the biological mother's request, the Bureau will not reveal her identity.*

Sometime before Kartya's arrival in Taiwan, on the 5th June 1998, with the massive coverage by the media, the Bureau received several calls from a woman (referred to as Mrs Chin in the following) who was heartbroken and kept weeping over the phone, asserting that Kartya was her biological daughter. Aside from claiming that she was a native of Taipei County, Mrs Chin would not leave any telephone number or personal particulars. We analysed the situation and thought that it was possible that she was the girl's biological mother. We not only tried our best to calm her down, but also urged her to keep close contact with the International Section of this Bureau.

On the ninth of this month (Tuesday) at about 5 o'clock in the afternoon, 'Mrs Chin' again contacted this Bureau, asking us to carry out a DNA comparison, though she was unwilling to have any media exposure.

According to 'Mrs Chin's' recollection, in September 1979, she and her de facto partner gave birth to their eldest daughter, then late the following year (1980) their second daughter was born. They did not report either of the births and therefore could not obtain residential registrations.

Four months after the birth of their second daughter, the birth father took the baby away, when the mother was absent from the house. Upon her return to the house, 'Mrs Chin' asked her partner, 'Where is the baby?' To her shock, the birth father said that because they were unable to financially afford to raise the baby girl, he had already placed her in somebody else's custody for a price of about 36,000 New Taiwan dollars.

Implored by 'Mrs Chin', the man went back several times to look for their second daughter, but was unable to find her whereabouts. Shocked and grief-stricken, 'Mrs Chin' left the man, taking her elder daughter with her. She continued for years to search for her baby daughter, but without success. The baby girl's birth father later died of alcohol poisoning. Now 'Mrs Chin' has formed a new family, and is very happy with her family life, and for that reason, does not want to reveal her identity. As to the physical condition of her second daughter, she said that during the four months following the baby's birth, she looked after her baby very well. The baby was not always healthy and often cried. She had a brown birthmark close to the corner of one of her eyes.

After comparisons being carried out several days in a row, this morning (16th) the Forensic Laboratory of the Bureau finally completed examining DNA of all the mothers who requested such an examination. The results showed that 'Mrs Chin' and her elder daughter's DNA matches that of Kartya. All others have been eliminated.

Thanks to the extensive coverage of this case by the media, 'Mrs Chin' was able to get in touch with this Bureau, and subsequently have her relationship with her daughter confirmed through DNA matching. For this reason, the Bureau wishes to thank the assistance provided by the media, and also the various sections of the community that showed their care in this case. The Bureau would like to take this opportunity to urge the public to care about society and to extend their love and help the missing ones be reunited with their families.'

CIB Taipei

The first thing that Kartya said after Mr Kay finished reading the press release was, 'That means I have a biological sister.' Mr

Kay turned and said, 'Yes, Kartya and you are an auntie. Your sister has a little baby. You also have two half sisters and two half brothers, all under twelve years.' Kartya looked stunned. She was speechless. Mr Kay started driving saying, 'We are going to meet them now.'

Kartya and I didn't speak during the trip to the CIB headquarters. As we arrived, Mr Kay told us to hide our heads. We lay down in the back seat. He drove through the police complex to a downstairs car park where he stopped and said, 'Keep down. I will be back in a minute.' When he came back, he apologised to us. He said that we could not meet the family tonight because the media had followed us and they were waiting out the front. The chief commissioner did not want the media present. The look of disappointment was all over Kartya's face. She was devastated. She would have to wait a bit longer before she saw her mother. Mr Kay drove us back to our hotel and said, 'I'm sorry. Maybe tomorrow.'

We were both exhausted, physically and emotionally. As we prepared to go to bed, I said to Kartya that we must talk to Christian Pirodon, the manager of the Imperial Inter.Continental, the next day. We had to see if we could extend our stay. They had been kind enough to sponsor us for ten days and today was day ten.

Kartya and I discussed what we had found out about her family. The main thing that had stayed in my mind was that her birth father had died of alcohol poisoning. You'd need a fairly heavy addiction to die from it at such a young age. Later we discovered he had been thirty-two. After all, this was what this journey was all about: to discover Kartya's background. To find out that her mother hadn't left her for dead. She wasn't the one who tied her down, abandoned her, gave her away. She had always loved her and had tried for years to find her. Her mother had been through all this pain as well.

Suddenly, I had such a feeling of love and warmth that it spread throughout my whole mind and body. I wanted to be able to put my arms around Kartya's mother and tell her that I loved her. She had shown courage and bravery to come forward. She had saved her daughter's life. I drifted into a sound peaceful sleep. I thought I was dreaming when I heard a knock on the door. At first I didn't get up, then I heard it again, only louder. I looked at the clock, it was 3.30 a.m. I jumped out of bed and ran to the door. I opened it and there stood Mr Kay. He said, 'You must come now, I will wait for you here.' I nodded. I went to wake Kartya. She was sound asleep. I shook her, 'Kartya, Kartya get up, we have to go.' She sat bolt upright in bed and said, 'Mum, are they kicking us out now?' She thought that we'd overstayed our time at the hotel and that we had to leave. I laughed, 'No silly, we're going to meet your mum.' We literally threw our clothes on. We didn't even brush our hair. Mr Kay took us down to his car still half asleep, and we went silently into the dead of night to the police headquarters.

We walked into the police gymnasium. It was a huge empty room, no chairs, just rubber mats on the floor. I held Kartya's hand. I was shaking all over and she looked petrified. We could see two women standing down the far end of the room. I didn't really see anyone else even though there were other people in the room. As we walked down to the two women, I focused only on them. As I approached the older woman, and was close enough to see her face, I suddenly felt like I'd been struck by lightning. It was her: the lady in my dream. It was her, no doubt at all. Kartya and I went towards them and then we stopped and just stood there. We didn't know what to do. I felt an overwhelming emotion and had a burning lump in my throat. It felt like a huge growth. A cry came out of my mouth. I instinctively walked to Kartya's mother and put my arms around her. I had never felt such emotion in my whole life. We were both crying and sobbing. I thought I would collapse. I was thinking, Othmar, where are you? I want you here. Kartya was holding her sister. They were both crying. I had never heard Kartya cry like that. It was a release of so many years of pain and sadness. Kartya's mother kept saying, 'Thank you, thank you.' I felt she was saying thank you for bringing Kartya back to the family. We kept hugging each other as if we both knew how the other felt.

This was the one we had been looking for; the one in my dream. This was the one I imagined all along. Just the reality of seeing her, this lady who had given birth to our daughter, was unbelievable. Her lovely face showed so much sadness and pain.

With my arms around her, I could feel her body trembling. This beautiful person who resembled our daughter. Kartya was still hugging her sister, stroking her cheek, scanning her face for any resemblance to herself. They could have been twins, they looked so alike. Her sister was looking up at her as if to say, where have you been all my life? I went over and put my arms around Kartya's sister. Kartya went and put her arms around her mother. Mother and daughter were reunited after seventeen years apart. Her mother cupped her face in her hands as if to say, you have returned. I was so happy for Kartya. For hours, time stood still. The four of us stood there with our arms around each other and cried. I thought to myself that this was it; this was the reward for so many years of pain and heartbreak.

It was all over. It had been worth all the pain to be part of this experience, this journey of discovery. To see our daughter with a look of total peace on her face. To see her mother and her sister with so much love in their eyes for the daughter and sister they lost, but never stopped loving, was worth everything. Her mother couldn't take her eyes off her. She didn't want to let her go.

We stood there for what seemed like hours, holding each other. Finally I realised there were other people in the room. Mr Kay then introduced us to Kartya's brother-in-law, Johnny, and her stepfather, Lontong. He told us that Kartya's mother's name was Li Meng and her sister was Jessie. Kartya asked Mr Kay to ask Li Meng if she had a Chinese name. Li Meng told her that she had been named little sister in Taiwanese. Mr Kay and other members of the CIB shook our hands and congratulated us. They had been moved to tears. Mr Kay said that the Chief Commissioner, Yang Tzu-Ching, would be down to speak to us. When he walked in, it was 5.20 a.m. He had a smile on his face from ear to ear.

He shook our hands warmly and enthusiastically. He introduced us to the forensic scientist who had conducted the DNA tests. She went through the procedure with us so that we understood how they had achieved a match. I wondered if any of them had slept at all. By the look of it, they had been dressed ready for the occasion all night. Kartya's mother and sister had gifts for us. A lovely watch and perfume each, and Kartya's mum gave her a beautiful gold necklace. When it came time to leave, we both felt very sad. We didn't know when we would see them again. We left them standing there and Mr Kay drove us back to our hotel. It was six-thirty in the morning.

I asked Kartya how she felt. She said, 'Mum, I didn't want to let go of my mum.' I said I understood. I hadn't wanted to let go of her either. Kartya went on to say, 'At that moment, when I held my mother, it just all went. All the pain and all the anger, it just went.' I knew what she felt like because her face had a look of peacefulness and serenity that I had never seen before. I put my arms around her and told her that we loved her, and that we always would. I felt a tinge of sadness for myself. I hoped that we hadn't lost her.

CHAPTER TWENTY-NINE
An Extended Family

We set out preparing our press conference to inform the media of the successful resolution of our search. At 10 a.m. we went to the conference room at the Imperial Inter.Continental to a huge reception from the media. The cameras and photographers were frantically trying to get all the photos they could. Firstly, Ian Hyslop thanked the press and all the people of Taiwan who helped us in our search. Everyone, though, just wanted to know how Kartya felt. I think the look on her face told them all they needed to know. She looked radiant. One journalist asked Kartya, 'Do you hate your birth mother for what happened to you?' Kartya said, 'No, I understand now what happened and I don't hate her at all.' Someone else asked her, 'What were your first thoughts when you first saw your mother?' Kartya answered, 'I looked at her and said, yes, that's my mother. I could feel it. She was no longer a big mystery in my life.' When a journalist asked me if I was now jealous because Kartya had found her birth mother, I said, 'No, not at all. Kartya can have two mothers, that's fine with us.' When someone asked Kartya what it felt like when she held her mother for the first time, she answered, 'At that moment, I felt so much love from my mother that all my pain went, it just all went.' There were tears in quite a few eyes as we got up to leave. We were going to the airport to pick up Othmar. We needed him to be with us.

Kartya literally jumped into her father's arms when she saw him. She was so happy to be able to share her happiness with him. Even at her most difficult times she had been able to retain a very close relationship with him. He made her feel like the new kid on the block. He treated her like an adult; it was me who still treated her like a kid. I sensed that was going to rapidly change. I couldn't help but wonder how she was going to feel about me, now that she had found what she had been looking for all her life. Was our relationship going to improve? After all, we had spent two weeks together without one fight. Surely that was a promising sign. I wanted so much to have the same sort of close relationship with Kartya as I had always enjoyed with Kiersten.

I told Othmar about the press conference and how Kartya handled herself with such courage and dignity under extreme emotional pressure. He said, 'That's doesn't surprise me, all those years on the streets must have been for some reason. It gave her the strength to reach out for her dreams.' I described for him my vivid dream about Kartya's mum and how, when I first set eyes on her, I knew it was her. The thing that was different was her hair. For some reason I imagined her to have long black hair like Kartya's, instead she had short, wavy brown hair. Othmar is quite spiritual about dreams. He believes that our dreams are real and that they can come true. He told me that he wasn't surprised that I had had an apparition. He said, 'The Lord works in mysterious ways. Maybe it was His way of giving us the strength to continue the search.' I wasn't going to disagree with that.

I told Othmar that Kartya's mother did not want to be identified to the media, but that we would be able to see her before we went back to Australia. Kartya's mum knew that Othmar was flying to Taiwan and she had expressed the wish to meet the man who had been her daughter's father. There were still lots of questions that we wanted to ask Kartya's mother, questions that we hadn't been able to ask at our 4 a.m. meeting. Kartya was still on a high and told Othmar, 'Dad, you should see my mum. She's just beautiful. And my sister looks like me.'

I was so happy to have Othmar with us. It would have been too hard to try and explain to him the sort of emotions involved on this whole journey if he hadn't have been able to come at all. Now we would be able to share our excitement and sense of achievement together. Othmar was suffering from jet lag and he was very tired. A good night's sleep would fix that—but not before Kartya told him everything that had happened so far. He said to me 'I've never seen her so happy, not ever. Makes you realise that it was all worthwhile. Everything was worth it in the end.'

The knock on our hotel room door at eight-thirty in the morning took me by surprise. I was still in bed asleep. Othmar was in blissful oblivion, snoring his head off, recovering from his jet lag. I opened the door. Mr Kay from Interpol was standing there. He said, 'You must come to CIB headquarters. I have encouraged Kartya's birth family to face the media. We must be there in fifteen minutes. I'll wait downstairs.' I woke Othmar and Kartya and we got dressed quickly. Othmar was still half asleep. It usually took him one hour to get himself ready, so he was feeling slightly disoriented. I was rushing him. He asked me what he should wear. I said, 'Anything, just hurry up.'

We hurried downstairs. I was feeling like I'd been dragged backwards through a bush and I probably looked like it as I had no time to put in my hot rollers or do my make-up. Othmar still looked half asleep. Kartya was the only one who appeared in control. No doubt she was excited about seeing her mum and sister again.

We got into Mr Kay's car and drove to the CIB. On the way, Mr Kay told us that he had spoken to Kartya's birth mother and encouraged her to meet the media. They were going to look for her anyway, so it was in everybody's best interests to go public. We could understand the media. It was natural that they would want to see mother and daughter reunited publicly. We went into a large room full of cameras and journalists. Kartya's mother and sister were sitting on big chairs with their backs to the cameras. I felt for them. This was very difficult for such a conservative, private family. They didn't want any publicity, but they didn't really have a choice.

The Chief Commissioner of Police, Yang Tzu-Ching, introduced Kartya's family to the media. Nobody asked us any questions this time, they were only interested in getting photos of the family together. Li Meng and Jessie seemed overwhelmed by the attention. Kartya stood between them, giving them support. Othmar and I put our arms around Kartya's mum. We were all crying again. I told her that I loved her. I kept saying, 'I love you, I love you.' Even though she didn't speak English, I'm sure she understood. Kartya had a protective arm around her sister and was holding her hand. You could see the vast contrast between them. Kartya, the Chinese kid brought up in Australia, tall, tough and fiercely independent, was very different to her older sister who had been brought up in Taiwan as a traditional Taiwanese girl. She was shorter than Kartya, very shy, very scared and overwhelmed by the whole experience.

That second meeting was just as emotional as the first. I think we were all still coming to terms with the enormity of what had happened. The fact that the miracle had happened was still unreal to us. We left the CIB with about forty cameras following us, falling all over each other for pictures. I felt so sad for Li Meng, Jessie and Kartya because they had not had a chance to be together privately. It had all been so public and I sensed their need to be together. As we walked out to get into Mr Kay's car, Othmar said, 'Has it been like this all week, the media attention?' I said, 'Yes, Othmar, yes it has, and it was all worth it.' He shook his head, overwhelmed by it all.

The phone in our hotel room hadn't stopped ringing. People from all over the world wanted to know the story of Kartya. We had calls from the BBC in London and from German television. Swedish and American television also called as, of course, did the Australian media. Everyone seemed to be elated and surprised that we had actually been successful. Adrian Brown, Asia correspondent for the Nine Network in Australia, arrived with two dozen yellow roses. Adrian had done some lovely reports on Kartya's story out of Taipei and we were touched by his caring approach. His unique sense of humour made us laugh. He told us that it was one of the nicer stories that he had worked on, and he was delighted that we had been successful. We thanked him for his support.

Ian and Kathy shared our sense of achievement. Their efforts had been monumental. They took on a huge challenge and worked tirelessly. Ian had been like a dog at a bone. He didn't give up for a second. The Australian team of 60 *Minutes* arrived to do a story on Kartya's reunion with her family. The presenter, Liz Hayes, and producer Stephen Taylor and their camera crew were staying at our hotel. Kartya related very well to Liz and Steven. Liz with her professional, yet casual approach appealed to Kartya. She was able to bring out the best in her. We all liked the quick-witted Stephen. He had a way of making the whole job seem easy and injected a *joie de vivre* into the occasion.

We were excited about the prospect of going to see Kartya's extended family. We all drove down to Chinsan, a coastal town about an hour's drive from Taipei where Kartya's family lived. It is a most beautiful part of the world, with ocean frontage and a mountain and ricefields backdrop. It was a steamy hot day and we were in an air-conditioned minibus with the *60 Minutes* crew. Poor Ian and Steve had to drive down in their car with no air-conditioning. They both resembled a grease spot when they arrived.

Kartya's mum lived in a condominium-style house on four levels. We walked into their home where there were about thirty of Kartya's relatives. They were all anxious to meet the long-lost family member from Australia. It was a bit overwhelming. There were aunties, uncles, cousins, grandparents and Kartya's two little half-sisters and two half-brothers. Kartya's sister, Jessie, and her little baby girl of about two months were present. Othmar and I were so proud to be able to reunite Kartya with such a wonderful family.

We learnt that Kartya's mum knew we were coming to Taiwan, even before we arrived. She had seen Kartya's story in the newspaper and instantly recognised the photo of the little fat-faced baby with the birthmark beside her eye. She had never forgotten the baby that was taken away from her seventeen years before. She had lived all those years with the guilt of blaming herself for what Kartya's birth father had done. She was also carrying a load of unresolved grief that could now be buried and put to rest. Kartya had only ever talked about finding her mother, she had never mentioned her father. Maybe it was best under the circumstances that her father wasn't around to answer any questions. Even when her mother told Kartya that there were over two hundred more family members for her to meet, it wasn't enough to knock the look of peace and serenity off her face; the face of this kid told the whole story.

CHAPTER THIRTY
The Circle is Complete

Othmar and I did wonder how Kartya was going to find her place in her new family, with its different language and culture. With us she was the youngest, the baby, the spoilt one. In her new family she would have to slot in the middle. We were confident, though, that it would work out. It would obviously take time and a lot of understanding on both sides. The whole family seemed to be excited about having an extra family member. The sharpest pair of scissors in the world could not have cut these ties, could not have erased this strong family bond. As I watched her squatting on the floor, eating her Chinese food, handling her chopsticks with the expertise of a local, I asked myself, how could we have not taken her on this journey? The thought that we might have denied this adopted child of ours her birthright did not bear thinking about.

By looking at this conservative Asian family, we could at last see our daughter for who she really was. Her birth mother had a way of conveying her emotions and feelings in an almost spiritual way, through her eyes, her face, her manner. Not at all demonstrative, like me. For years we had been concerned that Kartya was unable to physically demonstrate her love for us. We thought it was because she didn't love us. We now knew that was not the case.

Through meeting her birth family, we were able to understand Kartya in a way that we had never been able to before.

We were not going to lose Kartya to her birth family. Rather, in embracing this unique group of people our whole family would gain immeasurably. We had seen our daughter conduct herself with such courage and dignity that we were proud of this young Taiwanese girl, brought up in Australia. No-one was going to lose in this reunion.

When we completed filming for *60 Minutes* and they had left we all went out for dinner with Kartya's family. I talked nonstop with Kartya's mum. Poor Kathy was interpreting our every word. She told me that Kartya's birth father had a habit of squatting when he ate. The family resemblances were obvious. Kartya's mother had the same wide shoulders as Kartya, they both had long feet. Kartya's half-sister, Amy, who was eleven years old, was identical to Kartya at that age. She was outgoing and liked being the centre of attention. We loved her. It felt really strange being with all these people who bore a strange resemblance to 'our' daughter.

After a day that we will never forget, we went back to Taipei. Othmar and I sat in our hotel room and had a beer and talked about all the other mothers who had come forward and who would now be feeling sad. Sad that Kartya was not their daughter. Sad that they might never find out what happened to their babies. I really wanted to go to them and tell them that I would help them find their babies. I wanted to assure them that no matter where they had gone, they would have been loved and cared for.

I really hoped that through Kartya's story other adoptive families would help their children find their heritage. For us, it had been the most rewarding experience of our lives. For us, it was the reward after years of pain and sadness. It was the light at the end of the tunnel. It was better than winning the lottery. I hoped that the people of Taiwan understood that it took a lot of courage for Kartya to even attempt to try and find her mother. The pressure of the public scrutiny on her personally sometimes caused difficulties. After enduring years of feeling unwanted by her birth family, it wasn't easy for her to suddenly live up to everyone's expectations. The negative feelings she had built up over the years, the internalised battle she was waging, the fears that she was unworthy of anyone's love and affection, don't all just disappear overnight. It was going to take a lot of time for everything to fall into place. We knew that Kartya had feelings of apprehension that were causing her some concern. Just as she felt that she had not been able to live up to our expectations, naturally she was worried that she wouldn't live up to her birth family's expectations, either. That put a lot of pressure on her. She wanted to be able to satisfy the expectations that the media had placed on her, too, with personal appearances and television interviews. It was not an easy time for her. I couldn't help but analyse what had actually brought us to this point, to where we were in Taiwan supporting this young lady who was not our biological child, but was a child that we both loved with such a passion that made everything else unimportant. Was it our own upbringing that had taught us what it means to love another person unconditionally? Did that upbringing give us the strength and determination to continue the journey that many people would have given up on long ago? Or was it the simple fact that we didn't want to see a person we loved destroyed by influences that were out of our control? Othmar and I both wanted to see all of our children reach their full potential. Most of all, we wanted them to be happy with their lives. I knew that we were not the only family in the world that had walked the path of pain and hopelessness, even though, at times, we felt like we were. We had to believe that our ongoing love and support for Kartya would, in the end, bring about a resolution to the difficulties that our whole family was experiencing.

The easy thing would have been to walk away and not look back. We were not prepared to live with the feelings of guilt if we did that. We were not prepared to use Kartya's actions as a justification to our kids for not continuing to love and support her. We would have done the same for them if it was necessary. And because we had the support of Kiersten, Alex and Joshua, we couldn't let them down. They expected us to continue the journey, no matter where its final resting place was and, after six years, we felt we had finally found the end of the story. Another one was beginning, but this time it was going to be an easier journey; one we were all going to enjoy.

We wanted to show Othmar the night markets of Taipei. We went with Ian, Kathy and George Gao from *United Daily* newspaper. Kartya loved the markets; the masses of people out with their children at all hours of the night; the open-air shops and stalls crammed with clothes, handbags and shoes. It was like Disneyland for someone like Kartya, the shopaholic. Shopping was like another addiction for Kartya. You couldn't get her out of a shop without her buying something. Everywhere we went, we were recognised. People would call out 'Kia, Kia'. She loved being the centre of attention. I was 'Kia's mama', which made me feel pretty special.

We went into one shoe shop and the lady recognised Kartya. She was about to buy some more shoes to satisfy her shoe fetish. Kartya picked out two pairs and took them up to the owner. Not only would she not let us pay for them, she made me pick out a pair for myself free of charge. All the Taiwanese treated us like that, with genuine love and affection. Kartya now had eight pairs of new shoes. She had managed to squeeze enough money out of Stephen Taylor, from *60 Minutes*, to buy some shoes and George Gao was going to buy her a new pair of Nike sneakers. Kartya was never backwards in asking for what she wanted. She figured if you wanted something, you asked. She was always very upfront. If she wanted money, she would just ask.

Her birth mother, who also loved shoes, had given her some money that was burning a hole in Kartya's pocket. She bought some skirts, tops and pants, all the things she told me she really needed. She chose materials that were soft satin with a shiny finish. Kartya always loved running her hands over shiny fabrics. When she was tired she would hold a piece of fabric between her fingers and rub it together.

She picked out her new sneakers and George bought them. We all loved George, he had been instrumental in our success. He had become our friend and we had the utmost respect for him. George's elation at finding Kartya's family was evident; he couldn't wipe the smile off his face. He would say, 'It's amazing, just amazing.' He was a very proud man. George told me that he would get women ringing at the newspaper in tears wanting to know if Kartya's mother had been found. He said that the women of Taiwan had been deeply touched by the story. Othmar and I knew that when we left Taiwan we would miss all the new friends we had made, especially George.

The three weeks had seemed like three months. So much had happened and I would be very sad to leave. But we did have a big family to come back to for holidays, all two hundred of them. They really wanted us to come back, too. I was starting to feel a tinge of sadness, as well, because I knew that we would be going home without Kartya. We had discussed with Kartya before we left Melbourne that if she found her mother, she had our permission and blessing to stay in Taiwan for as long as she wanted to. She was old enough to make the decision when and if she wanted to return home. Othmar was not worried. He said, 'Don't worry, she'll be back home when she's ready. She's the Velcro villain, remember.'

Kartya was looking forward to staying in Taiwan, being with her birth family, trying to build a relationship with them. She knew that it would take time, that it wouldn't be easy. I had said to her, 'Kartya, you have not been with them for seventeen years. Even if it takes five years to establish a firm bond with them, it's worth it.' She knew also that even though she loved Taiwan, we were not going to be with her, and she was going to get very homesick.

At the hotel, we were sent some lovely letters and cards of congratulations from people all over Taiwan. One card that Kartya received touched us both to tears.

Dear Kartya We feel so happy to read from the newspaper that you've finally found and met your own mother and sister. It is such a great gift from God. We learn that you suffered a lot, hoping to know who you are and where you came from. Now that you've got the answer, the pain pays off. Here is a souvenir I bought four years ago. I would like you to have it. This glass shoe has a symbolic meaning. In the fairytale of Cinderella, the handsome prince tried everything he could do to find the girl who he danced with at the ball, with the help of the glass shoe, he found her. In your story, you yell in a deep corner of your heart to meet your own mother someday in your life. With voices of prayer, you found her. A new life experience is waiting for you ...

Love Daisy

The love and sincerity with which all these letters were written touched us deeply. We were also honoured to receive letters from the Governor of Taiwan, one to Kartya and one to us. Ours read:

Mr and Mrs Wunderle, The news of the success of your quest to help Kartya was

most heartwarming. You have proven your love for your adopted daughter. Often, conditions thwart us, but the perseverance of the human spirit, and the ability to overcome awesome obstacles, motivates us not to give up. I applaud your persistence over seventeen years and your unselfish determination to help your daughter to achieve a deep rooted ambition. What a great gift you have given your daughter. I must say, that you have set an example for the people of this country, and indeed the whole world. Your presence in Taiwan is most appreciated. I offer you an official welcome to many happy visits in the future.

James C. Soong Governor Taiwan

It was clear to us that the people of Taiwan understood Kartya's strong need to go back to the beginning to unearth the truth of her past. The Chinese, of all people, understand this. They did not see her as a rebellious adolescent but as a person who needed to walk the path to complete the circle. Now a new journey was going to begin for Kartya and for the two families that loved her.

We had had her company for seventeen years, now it was her birth mother's turn to get to know her daughter.

I could only imagine the deep sense of loss that Kartya's mother must have felt for all those years; never knowing where her child was nor if she was alive or dead; looking for her in every face she saw. There is not a mother in the world who would not understand how she had felt. I was glad that I had always stuck by my belief that Kartya's mother did not give her up. I simply never believed that a mother would give up such a beautiful, healthy baby.

The time had now come for Othmar and me to leave our daughter where she belonged. I was not prepared to entertain the thought that she wouldn't come home. I had a gut feeling that, given time, she would realise that her ties with us, her adoptive family, were stronger than she realised. Just as we had not turned our back on her, we believed that she would not turn her back on us.

We all sat in Malibu West, an American-style restaurant that we had often visited during our three weeks in Taiwan. When we wanted a change from Chinese food, Ian would take us there. We'd eat spaghetti bolognaise or club sandwiches and chips, and Ian and Kartya would play pool. We'd listen to Kenny Rodgers singing 'The Gambler' or Patsy Cline singing 'I Fall to Pieces'. The final day that song was playing again, and inside I was falling to pieces. I tried to stop myself from bursting into tears. We sat and had a beer together, Ian, Kathy, their daughter Morgan, Julie Chu and her husband Tony, Eddie Song, a reporter with the *China Post*, Kartya's brother-in-law, Johnny, Kartya and her mum, Othmar and myself. We were all packed, ready to get on the plane and fly home. Kartya was sitting next to her mother, holding her hand. She looked so happy. I felt so sad. I even felt a tinge of jealousy: she would never hold my hand. Eddie kept asking me if I was crying. I told him no. I had my dark sunglasses on; no-one was going to see my eyes. I had a lump in my throat that was threatening to burn a hole in my neck. I was emotionally drained. Othmar was holding my hand. I had to be strong for Kartya. I knew she wanted to stay, but I knew she would miss us and I didn't want to make it any harder for her by losing control. The thought of getting on the plane was making me breathe shallowly. Eddie asked me again if I was crying yet. I said no. If I had let go of my emotions, my tears would have washed me away into the gutters of Taipei. I looked at Kartya's beautiful mother. I could tell by her eyes that she knew how I felt.

We all got up and left to go to the airport. When we arrived, I pulled Julie Chu aside and told her that no matter what anyone said, I believed what she did was in the best interests of Kartya. Nothing that had happened over the past three weeks had changed my mind about that. She had suffered, paid her penance to the children, to society and to herself. I hugged her and told her that I loved her. Othmar and I both thanked Ian and Kathy. We had no words to convey our feelings, all we could say was thanks for all the work. Othmar and I were standing there. He was holding my hand, squeezing it as if to say, Don't worry, it will be fine. I was thinking there was a strange irony about the situation. My thoughts took me back to Melbourne airport seventeen years before when we were standing together awaiting the arrival of our baby. Now we were leaving her in the country she left, with the mother who lost her, seventeen years before.

Kartya pulled me aside, wrapped her arms around me and, through her tears, said, 'Mum, none of this would have happened without you and Dad. I love you both and I will never forget what you have done for me. I am truly sorry for all the pain I put everyone through.' We were both crying. I didn't want to let go of her because, for the first time, she wanted to hug me. She didn't tense up. The brick wall was gone. I hoped that maybe in finding her birth family, she had in turn found us, her adoptive family. I said to her, 'Kartya, be a good girl for your mother. Come back home to us one day, we'll be waiting for you. Don't forget about us.' I told her that I loved her. I put my arms around her birth mother. I told her that I loved her, too. I said, 'I know you will look after our daughter.' I don't know if she understood me, but the tears in her eyes told me that she did. Kartya hugged Othmar. They were both crying. He made a sign of the cross on her forehead. He grabbed my hand and we walked away. I didn't look back. I couldn't. My mind kept saying over and over, a poem that I had written months before.

You and Me

We'll find this birth mother, you and me
to unlock your heart and set you free
To take away the pain you feel inside
feelings of anger, no need to hide
I hear your tears behind your door
getting louder and louder
I can't take much more
Together, we'll go, hand in hand
to search for her
in an unknown land
Your dream will come true, of that I'm sure
she'll be waiting for you, this birth mother of yours
With open arms, to hold you tight
to soothe your pain and make it right
But just remember, when you do
not to forget
I'm your mother, too.

As Othmar and I buckled up our seatbelts on the plane, I opened a letter that Kartya had given me just before we left.

Dear Mum and Dad, Looking back over the past six years together, I could not imagine being with a better family. Not once did you ever think of giving up on me. I could not be more thankful to you. As I look at it now, I have TRULY found myself. I can now live a positive life, with all my past in the blurred background. You never gave up on me, and I couldn't or don't want to imagine where I would be now if you didn't stick by me. You pulled me through everything and now I have finally found out all these answers to my life. It was a struggle, but we finally got there. Without your support, I wouldn't know what I would have done. For one thing, I know I would be dead by now if I didn't make the Journey of Discovery. I love you both so much for helping me through the roughest time in my life, I will love you always.

Your daughter of Taiwan, Kartya

With tears in my eyes, my sweaty hands gripped the seat as we flew over Taiwan and I imagined we were going to finish up at the bottom of the South China Sea.

CHAPTER THIRTY-ONE
Too Much Information

$\mathcal{I}$ don't know how one is supposed to feel after leaving a much loved daughter with her birth mother. I know I was not jumping over the moon. The image of Kartya, with her arms wrapped around her mother, farewelling us at Chiang Kai-shek Airport in Taipei, gave us some comfort. This was what we all wanted; some peace, some sense of the last few years of pain and heartache. I wondered how she would cope with all her new-found information. I wondered how we would cope without Kartya.

Maybe we could start to live like a 'normal' family? The family we all dreamed of being. But nothing was going to be the same, nothing ever is.

It was time for the other kids. Kiersten, Alex and Joshua. They had stood by, while all our time and energy went into helping Kartya.

For the next few months we enjoyed each other's company in

peace and quiet, without any dramas. Kartya rang every couple of days, sounding very chirpy and positive. We were all glad she sounded so happy. Othmar was at peace. He felt that all the hard times were over. I was not feeling as elated as I hoped I would be. I ached all over. My gums ached. It felt like someone had taken all my teeth out with a pair of pliers. My head ached. My stomach ached. I wished I could just let go of her and not continually worry about her. I hated myself for being an emotional "misfit". Why couldn't I be stronger?

When Kartya rang and told us that her mum was bringing her to Australia for her 18th birthday we were overjoyed. We were all very excited about seeing Kartya, her mum, her young sister Aimee and her cousin Josie. What a beautiful gesture it was of Kartya's mum to want to come and see where her daughter had grown up. When they all arrived in Melbourne we took them back to our house and I cooked chicken schnitzels, bratkartoffel and salad. Poor Josie was flat out translating for us as her English was impeccable. I could feel a definite warmth between myself and Kartya's mum, we did a lot of smiling and touching, bonding between two mothers. We could see that Kartya was very happy in the company of her family, even though communication was frustrating for them, they managed to understand each other with a lot of gesturing and hand signs. As they were only staying for a week, we made the most of the time by showing them around Melbourne. We took them down to Geelong to meet my dad. He was alone since my mum had died. He had followed Kartya's story with immense interest. He once said to me, "Nola, I don't know how you found her. I would have said it was impossible, it was a big surprise to me." Dad was over the moon to meet Kartya's mum. He thought she was a beautiful lady. I wished my own mum had been alive to experience the miracle. She would have loved every minute of it. Young Aimee offered to stay in Geelong and care for my dad. She was very sweet, sitting at the table, holding my dad's hand. My dad was very touched with their visit and he was also happy to see Kartya again. After a whole day spent with our family in Geelong, we drove back to Melbourne to celebrate Kartya's birthday. We all went out for yum cha, Kartya's favourite food. She was in her element being the centre of attention, getting presents and money on her special day. The next day they all left to go back to Taiwan. Kartya was returning with them indefinitely. Othmar and I felt that she needed to spend as much time as possible with her Taiwanese family. It had to be all about Kartya and her mum. They needed the time to re-establish the mother child bond, if that was possible after 18 years apart: a separation that probably should have never happened in the first place.

I had gained so much knowledge about what had happened in Taipei all those years ago. I had collected lots of news stories and spoken to people involved in the 'Julie Chu adoptions'.

It all started in 1979 when a woman called Chin Shu-hua adopted a baby girl. She had originally planned to raise the child herself, and offered NT$8000 (approx $300) to a doctor at the Chung-shan Obstetric Clinic to issue a falsified birth certificate to the effect that she was the natural mother of the child. Some time later she discovered she was pregnant and decided she no longer wanted her adopted child. She knew of a lawyer, whose office arranged for the adoption of Chinese children overseas. When she made inquiries, she met Chu Li-ching (Julie) who worked as secretary in that office, and Julie undertook to help her arrange for the baby to be adopted overseas. From that time on, Chin Shu-hua and Julie cooperated in arranging for unmarried mothers, and other mothers who for special reasons could not raise their own children, to have their babies adopted overseas. They arranged introductions and dealt with the formalities, and received a large amount of money from these activities. They agreed between them that Chin would be responsible for advertising their services in the classified columns of the newspapers and that Julie would be responsible for falsifying birth certificates, arranging adoption papers through the courts and obtaining exit permits for the children.

Their arrangement proved to be both successful and lucrative. Over three years it expanded to include a number of people, some knowingly involved in the illegal aspects and some unwittingly. Friends, family, medical professionals and strangers were recruited to falsify birth certificates and legal documents; obtain fraudulent registrations by impersonation and provide 'low cost' temporary care of the children. Mothers (and in some cases fathers and grandparents) who wished to relinquish their children were paid and arrangements made for the babies to be adopted to overseas parents who were unaware of the circumstances. The group, apart from arranging approximately forty legal adoptions (i.e genuine birth certificates, genuine parents and genuine household registration), illegally arranged the adoptions of thirty five children.

Julie and her co conspirators (including her then fiancé Lin Wen-chung (Tony) were eventually discovered, tried by the local Taipei court and convicted of criminal charges. Julie, appealing against her sentence of life imprisonment, took the matter to the Supreme Court. Whilst the Supreme Court upheld the rulings relating to falsification of records, and advertisement of and involvement in, illegal activities, other aspects of the criminal charges could not be proven — specifically those relating to coercion and the 'infringement of the natural rights of the family'. In reading through the files of all thirty five children adopted overseas, the court found there was not a single case in which an attempt was made to forcibly remove a child from their families. Nor was there any evidence that the accused used any force or threats in order to obtain the children, nor was there any sign that they took advantage of another's misfortune to get them. Many witnesses testified in court to the effect, "The natural mothers of the children were unmarried mothers, they wanted to have their children adopted and it was alright to send them overseas." There was a large number of letters on the files which showed that Julie had records of the whereabouts of all the children adopted overseas, some of them having been authenticated by diplomatic missions. These records showed that the children were in excellent health, both psychologically and physically. There were also about twenty colour photographs of the children showing that those children were living with good families. The Supreme Court partially cancelled the appellant's original sentences.

Whilst the Supreme Court also ruled there had been no infringement on the rights of the children or their freedom by sending them overseas for adoption I can't help but wonder how the now adults of the Julie Chu fraudulent adoptions feel about losing their mothers, family, country, heritage, culture and so much more.

Altogether six individuals were tried and found guilty of acts detrimental to certain families and other matters against the Criminal Code. The original case was heard in the Taipei local court on February 28th 1982 which sentenced Julie Chu to life imprisonment. They then appealed to the Supreme Court. The original sentence was partially cancelled and Julie was finally sentenced to six years imprisonment, Mrs Chen to five years imprisonment and Tony Lin to two years and six months imprisonment. Several other individuals also served prison sentences for their part in the crime.

We as a family had always known about the trial of Julie Chu. Somehow we always felt that our adoption of Kartya was legal. That's what we wanted to believe. As it turned out, we had been tricked as well.

CHAPTER THIRTY-TWO
Come Back Home

We had been getting mixed reports from Taiwan about Kartya's behaviour, some saying that she was doing well, and other reports saying she was not coping. I knew things were not good when I got a phone call, reverse charges from a 7-11 store, from Kartya crying, "Mum, I've had a fight with my mum and I'm not going back, what will I do?" I immediately phoned Ian Hyslop, the Australian journalist who had helped us find Kartya's family. He said Kartya could stay with him and Kathy in Taipei until she sorted things out with her mum. I felt the peace we had experienced for three months would soon be coming to an end.

After a couple of weeks with Ian and Kathy, things took a turn for the worse. It was a letter from Ian that made us realize we had to bring Kartya home.

Dear Nola,

It seems like a lifetime ago that you "blokes" were over here on that "magical mystery" tour that turned so many lives upside down and touched so many people.

I want you to know how Kartya and her birth mother's relationship has panned out over the past few months. This you have been hearing from all parties, however, as I put pen to paper and as we've had limited time to talk at length about it, let me make some observations that may fill in some holes.

First, needless to say, there's no one who understands Kartya better than you. So it's a safe assumption that you'd be aware she cuts a less than sympathetic figure to those cast in the role of guardian, protector, birthmother, stepfather, female translator or jealous siblings.

It was always going to be hard bringing together a troubled kid reared in the west and the traditional Chinese mother with a new family.

Simply put....Kartya was dragged under the microscope by all of them and failed the test. Years of living "feral" and doing drugs has predictably left the kid incapable of displaying any concern or consideration for anyone but herself.

Kartya's chances of winning unconditional acceptance were slim from the start.

Well...I know this is an all too familiar story as you've had to cope with Kartya's addiction, mood swings and general all-round disposition. But frankly, her behaviour was a bit of a shock to us novices in the area of teenage rearing.

So, what is it I'm trying to say?....The biggest problem is her drinking. While it's simple to say alcohol is an obvious substitute for drugs, I've come across her....not that she knows it...in the early hours in front of the T.V. getting tucked into either a bottle of scotch or brandy. I've subsequently found out from a number of friends that she's also left the house after midnight while we slept, and gone drinking.

These facts I relate to you, not to dump on the kid.....as hurt as I personally feel about some of her actions, I want you and Othmar to be aware of the drinking problem so you are prepared to deal with it and the possibility of Kartya finding her former friends and resorting to the old habit.

Your relationship with Kartya has never been better. Now is the time to capitalize on that. I have no doubt she has grown up a good deal over here. She's certainly better off for the experience and hopefully aware she's now the only one who can truly control her own destiny.

There have been positive spots. Kartya has become more confident and capable of handling people and the media.

But Nola, I have to say, had she played it smarter, things could have turned out differently. Then again, use the word "played it" pretty much sums it up. Kartya finds it very difficult to be anything but herself. Some may say, why should she?

I'm afraid, however, if she doesn't try harder in the future, she'll continue to encounter problems and resort to quick fixes to alleviate the pain.

It's a pain that you initially explained to me as a confused kid with an identity crisis. It has however, proved to be much more complicated than that.

Please accept everything I say, including points that maybe interpreted as a criticism of Kartya, are made to help you understand what's been happening to your daughter in Taiwan over the past few months.

None of this is said to hurt Kartya or your family. It's simply an attempt on my part to fill you in on some of the dynamics of her stay here, and the fact is we all are seriously concerned about Kartya's future.

The bottom line is Kartya is now of legal age and yet she has never been more vulnerable. We've discussed it many times, Nola, and I guess you're saying to yourself, I should have had a better idea of what to expect. That's probably right. But knowing how hard I have tried, having to write this letter is tinged with sadness because we still very much want Kartya to look forward to a good future.

She has come so far in recent months, for her to return to Australia and the old habits would be as they say in the classics "a crying shame".

Please accept the spirit in which this letter was written,

Best Regards.......Ian

We could understand where Ian was coming from, he was a bit out of his depth with Kartya. Apart from the fact that she was a heroin addict, a lot of her behaviour was not unlike a lot of teenagers who can be pretty revolting even when they are essentially good. To be confronted with her anti-social behaviour and her moods would have been too much to expect Ian and his family to understand. All the pain of the past was not going to disappear overnight. Of course there was going to be enormous adjustments for Kartya and her mum.

We could not expect them to continue to keep her safe. The time had come for her to return home. To come back where she belonged, with us, her 'real family', and we felt the sooner the better.

Kiersten, Alex and Josh were happy she was coming home. Despite everything that had happened over the years, they still missed her and loved her.

I felt quite excited driving to the airport to pick her up. I was optimistic about the future, and even though we had all come a long way, I knew in my heart we still had a long way to go.

Kartya came out of the arrival doors, I threw my arms around her, and she hugged me. She looked fantastic, very happy and glad to be home.

We spent the next few weeks catching up on all the news. Just before she left Taiwan, Kartya saw her mum again and things between them were resolved. They promised to keep in touch with each other. Having been re-united with them was just the start, now the healing on both sides could begin in earnest.

Kartya and Josh were living at home with Othmar and I. Kiersten was living in a unit with a girlfriend, and Alex was also living independently. The first few weeks Kartya was at home was spent catching up with all her friends. She was always out and about socialising. People were drawn to her like a magnet. She had the ability to manipulate and control any situation to suit her. Othmar and I wanted her to do something productive with her time, maybe get a job or go back to school.

For the next couple of years Kartya lived in and out of home. Was she still using drugs? Mostly, I didn't know. I didn't want to know. Drugs had exhausted us mentally and physically, so I didn't want to go down that road again. I knew Kartya was on and off the methadone program and I felt a bit of comfort in that. She was no longer a twelve-year old and I had to accept that she was now making her own decisions. She was no longer angry with me for being her mother. I think she was actually quite happy I was. Othmar and I were working very hard most of the time. I was working every day, and driving to and from work took three hours out of my day, so I felt deprived of time and was exhausted at the end of each day. I made sure I cooked a decent meal every day for myself and Josh. I always plated one up for Kartya if she popped in. Othmar ate at work.

Joshua was working hard and I wanted to try and spend some time with him. He was the one who was always there for me, through thick and thin. When I was a wreck through stress, he never failed me. He would put the vegetables on at night. Take the clothes off the line. Vacuum the house. Anything he could do to help me, he did.

With Othmar at work every night, I would not have survived without the physical and emotional support from Josh. He was with me all the time. I really worshipped the ground he walked on. I felt a lot of guilt about not having the time to be there for him when he had spent most of his adolescence worrying about Kartya. Kiersten and Alex were the same, worrying about Kartya and trying to support us as well.

There was still a lot of media interest in Kartya and her story. She did a lot of interviews for newspaper and television reports. She was always very honest about her life and her addiction and we were very proud of her. She stood up and told the truth in the hope that it would help other young people with addictions.

It was when I got a letter from a young girl called Allisha that I realised we were not alone.

Dear Nola and Kartya,

I feel compelled to write to you to tell you both how your story changed my life. My name is Allisha. I am the middle child of three children. I am very pretty or so I am told. I am very smart and I am a heroin addict. You may well ask, if I am so smart, then why I am using heroin.

This is my story.

I have had a private education since kindergarten. I don't know exactly when or why things started to go wrong for me, but they did. Initially, I started in year 10 smoking marijuana. At every party I went to all the kids smoked it, it seemed normal and acceptable. One day someone offered me heroin to smoke. Thinking that my friends were smoking it, I decided to try it for fun. Eventually I was injecting it. One day my parents found a syringe in my room and they went crazy. I was feeling so depressed and lonely and very, very angry. My parents were screaming and yelling at me, wanting to know why I was using drugs. How could I give them an answer when I didn't know myself? I decided to leave home. I knew that if I got angrier with my mother and blame her, she would then ask me to leave, which is exactly what happened. I became homeless. I mixed with other people who were using. They became my "family". I lived in a Salvation Army youth refuge, which I hated. I just wanted to go back home, but how could I when they were all so angry with me? I had let them down. I had hurt them and I wasn't living up to their expectations of me. Like most drug addicts, I had become very selfish. Thinking only of myself and my pain. When I read all the articles about Kartya and then saw you on 60 minutes, I couldn't stop crying because it was if I was reading my own story. I had not seen my mother for seven months. I didn't think she wanted to see me. Even though she knew where I was living, she never came to see me. I read in the newspaper that you, Nola, kept your relationship with Kartya by writing her letters and she wrote back to you in a way that she was unable to verbalise face-to-face. I sat down and wrote to my family. I tried my best to tell them how I was feeling. How I felt so much pain and I didn't want to live without them. I asked them for help. I put my letter in an envelope and on the front I wrote, To dear Mum, Dad, Ben and Aimee. Please don't hate me, love from Allisha.

My counsellor from the refuge drove to my parent's home and gave it to them. I can honestly tell you that I did not expect to hear from them. Last week, three days after sending my letter, my mum turned up at the front door of the refuge. She had tears streaming down her face. She put her arms around me and for the first time in nearly a year, she said, "Allisha, we love you, please come home."

I cannot tell you what that meant to me, Kartya. I guess it was a bit like when you held your mum for the first time. I went and packed my bags and my mum took me home. I have agreed to go on the methadone program and to have counselling. I don't know what the future holds, but I do now feel that I will have a future. I just wanted to know my family loved me, because of all the pain I had put them through, I certainly didn't love myself. Kartya, you showed such bravery in coming forward about your problems, and it was your openness and honesty that had a huge impact on me. I wanted you to know that your story changed my life. It made my family realise I had an illness and was not a bad person. I now feel with their love and support I will make it. Hopefully I can resume my education. I need to get well first. I would like to be a probation officer so I can help young kids get back on track. After all I have been through, I think

I would be good at it. All my love to you both and I hope one day Kartya will write her story.

Love from Allisha

I cried when I read Allisha's letter. It made me feel so sad. Sometimes the pain is just too much to bear for drug addicts and their families.

Unfortunately heroin addiction was a taboo subject. No-one wanted to talk about it. Certainly don't admit that you had a child with the addiction. This was at a time when our major newspaper highlighted every day the deaths from heroin as against the deaths from car accidents. Overdoses far outweighed the road toll every day. It was at this time that I met and became firm friends with a man named John Robinson. He had heard about Kartya's story and contacted me. He was struggling with a family member with addiction. I found him to be inspirational in that he wasn't ashamed to talk about heroin addiction and I loved him because he thought Kartya was wonderful. We thought of all sorts of ways to deal with addiction. We organised get together's with other parents facing the same crisis. There were numerous occasions when I rang John for help or advice and he was always there. This is priceless when most people don't want to know about it. John and his wife Lyn have played a huge role in our lives and especially Kartya's.

CHAPTER THIRTY-THREE
Fresh Start

Kartya settled back at home with us. She had a lot of plans about her future. One of the biggest problems she had with her family in Taiwan was her inability to communicate. It's too difficult to convey feelings when you are not speaking the same language. Kartya was on the methadone programme. It seemed to keep her addiction under control and help her get on with her life. I think she was disappointed that she didn't feel the deep connection with her mother that she yearned for. We did tell her that it could take many years for a bond to develop. You can't take a child from her mum and a mum from her child and then put them back together 18 years later and expect it all to work out. The pain, the loss, the grief, the guilt is still all there. The feelings of abandonment and lack of trust can affect an adoptees life forever. Only a mother and child know how this feels.

It didn't take Kartya long to catch up with all her friends and pick up her social life where she left it before going to Taiwan. Kartya wanted to learn Mandarin, so she enrolled in a TAFE course. We got her all the books she would need to study and paid the school fees. She seemed committed to learn and we hoped that it would help her get back on track. After a couple of weeks, she met a young boy called Rhett. Her studying went out the window. Flew away like a little bird. She started spending all her time at Rhett's house. We were not too concerned about her reverting to drug use, because she was stable on methadone. I would often go and visit her at his house and have a glass of wine with his mum. Kartya was quite happy there. She would come home on occasions, have a meal and then leave again. When she told us she was pregnant we were shocked. She was not stable enough to be a mother. She still had a lot of issues to work through. When she told me that Rhett's mum was taking her for a termination I felt very sad. Even though at the time, it was the right choice for Kartya to make, it was still a painful decision for her to make. She was not ready to be a mum herself. It was difficult for her to sustain a relationship when she still had lots of unresolved feelings of abandonment. When she got close to someone, those feelings came back and she would move on. Run away and start all over again with someone else.

It was quite some time later that she met a young man named Sascha. He was half Indian and half Croatian. He was a lovely boy, very warm and caring and he adored Kartya. They rented a unit together for about a year. It was during this time that Kartya got the methadone monkey off her back. She was clean for the first time in years. She was healthy, happy and enjoyed being a homemaker, cooking, cleaning, living in domestic bliss.

They seemed very happy together. Sascha worked every day

while Kartya stayed home and cooked. I would visit her and she would have everything prepared for the evening meal.

They would often visit Sascha's family for a meal. His mother didn't like Kartya very much and she felt it. She didn't feel very welcome at all. Cracks started to appear in the relationship, Kartya told me that she wasn't happy and was going to leave.

When her relationship with Sascha broke down, Kartya packed up her furniture and all her belonging's, and put them in storage. It was only a matter of weeks when she started a relationship with a Vietnamese boy. His name was Tri. Some nights she wouldn't come home, she would stay over at his place. Before long, she was living with him. He lived with his parents and siblings. We didn't think it was all that serious, their relationship, but Othmar and I hoped that he wasn't a drug user. Kartya's first Vietnamese boyfriend Tran had introduced her to drugs in the first place. Sadly, he died of a drug overdose. When we met Tri, he seemed a likeable young man, so we tried not to worry about her too much. Although we did suspect at times that they were on something. I have to be honest and say that in my heart I knew they were using. I never wanted to ask her because I didn't want her to tell me she was. Only a parent of a drug user will relate to how we felt at the time. When you have absolutely no control over a situation it is easier to put it out of your mind. I am sure a stronger person would have confronted it head on. I wanted to pretend everything was normal. Kartya was twenty years old. She was old enough to make her own life and choices. It had been two years since she was reunited with her mum in Taiwan. They had not had any contact since then. It was just too hard. At that time not many people had a computer or the internet. I was sure that one day Kartya would meet her family again and their reunion would have a positive outcome in the end.

Kartya and Tri visited us several times while they were together. He came across as a very young boy just having fun. When I would ask her if everything was alright, she would just say yes. She wouldn't have told me if she was using drugs. Kartya was no longer on methadone, so she had no safety net to curb her addictions. Othmar and I felt that the sooner they finished whatever relationship they had, the better.

CHAPTER THIRTY-FOUR

Mum I'm Pregnant

~~~

Kartya's relationship with Tri was over. She wanted to come back home. When she asked me to take her to the doctor to go back on methadone, I knew that they both had been using. Othmar and I were happy she was back with us. We felt she had a better chance of managing her addiction while living in a safe, stable environment.

When Kartya announced, "Mum I'm pregnant," I didn't know whether to laugh or cry. Firstly, she was on methadone and she wouldn't be getting off that overnight. We were not that confident that she was physically and emotionally ready to take on the roll of a mother. I was torn between thinking yes, this will be good, to no, this is bad. Of course the decision was Kartya's and she wanted to have her baby. All we could do was support her choice. The family were happy for Kartya, they all supported her. Of course the negative element crept in with well meaning people commenting on her having a 'methadone' baby. We were all actually very proud of Kartya for going forward with her decision to be a single mum. It was not going to be easy, but with help we all felt she could make it work. Kartya had a great midwife who had a lot of experience with mums on methadone. She understood Kartya and was very professional in giving her all the information she needed to prepare herself for the possibility that her baby could be born methadone dependant.

When Kartya was six months pregnant she moved into a unit with Kiersten. It was a good start for Kartya because she would have a nice place to bring her baby home to and Kiersten was there to help her. Without the love and support of her sister, Kartya would have struggled. She had very little contact with the father of her baby during this time, although he did know she was pregnant.

We talked to Kartya about who she wanted to support her during delivery. Kartya was happy for Kiersten and myself to be there. The three of us were all very close and had been through a lot together. So when Kiersten rang me in the early hours of the morning, "Mum, she's in labour," I knew it was time to go to the hospital. It's funny when someone goes into labour, everyone panics and thinks the baby will be born then and there. That rarely happens, and as in Kartya's case it took forever. Kiersten and I were in the labour room for about 15 hours. Kartya was screaming and yelling for pain relief. Eventually they gave her an epidural and a look of peace came over her face. It was awful watching her go through so much pain and not be able to help her. Kiersten and I took turns rubbing her back, trying to make her feel comfortable. Sometime in the late evening, Othmar turned up. He had been at work all day and was calling in to see what was happening. Not long after, the midwife and nurses came in and started Kartya pushing. Low and behold, after a couple of pushes, the head emerged. I thought I was going to pass out. It was such an amazing experience to watch the birth of our first grandchild. Othmar, Kiersten and I were overwhelmed with love for this beautiful, perfect little baby girl. How proud we were of Kartya. She had a reward at the end. The lovely Isabella Mei-Lin Wunderle. She had lots of visitors coming to see her and her new baby. Isabella's father, Tri, came into the hospital with his parents and sisters. He had a nurse and cuddle and left. They have had no contact since then. Kartya recovered very quickly after the birth and was able to go home after a week. Unfortunately, Isabella had to stay in hospital for another 55 days while she was weaned off the effects of being born with methadone in her system. Kartya went to the hospital every day to be with her baby. It was very exhausting for her and she was worried about not being with her all the time. Tiny Bella got stronger each day and did not appear to be stressed. She was actually very calm and was feeding and behaving very well. Kartya was over the moon when she was able to take her baby home. She was all prepared for the new arrival and had everything she needed to take care of a new baby.

With the help of Kiersten and the rest of the family she settled down to being a single mum to Bella. She quickly got into a routine with bathing and feeding and Bella thrived. Othmar and I would visit as often as we could. We were both working full time so it was mainly weekends that we got to have little Bella for a sleep over. She was such a perfect baby. Lyn and John Robinson also cared for Bella to give Kartya a break. John would take Bella shopping in the stroller. Lyn would get Bella in bed with her, so she could lie down and just look at her. Everyone just adored Bella. It was not long after Bella's first birthday that we noticed Kartya was struggling. She was a perfectionist and wanted everything to be perfect and expected perfection from herself. In her strive to be the best mum she could be she put unrealistic pressure on herself. She was finding it too difficult to care for Bella and her own health at the same time. She asked for help. I was at work every day. Kiersten was also. Othmar had retired from work as his health wasn't 100%. He offered to take care of Bella during the day and I would take over when I got home from work. Kartya knew that we would do whatever it took to make it less painful for her and Bella. Kartya came every day to see Bella and help bath and feed her. Othmar would smear her all over with Amolin. With her shiny greasy face, Bella looked like a little Buddha. Othmar loved it. He would take Bella shopping with him. They would go to the park in the afternoon or to the lake to feed the ducks. Then back home to bed for Bella with 'Opera Without Words' softly playing in the background. About three months later when Kartya was feeling stronger and more able to cope, Bella went home with her mum. She was 15 months old. Othmar had done such an amazing job, with such perfect routine, we were all so proud of him. Now that Kartya was a mum herself she was thinking she would like to go and visit her own mum in Taiwan. She was proud of her beautiful Bella and wanted to introduce her to her Taiwanese grandmother. Financially it would be a strain, but I promised Kartya that when we had the money, I would take her back. We felt she needed to re-connect with her mum, this time on a different level. In the meantime Kartya met another Vietnamese boy. His name was Sam. They started going out, eventually moving in together.

We saved over the next few months and finally had enough money to organize our trip back to Taiwan. We booked tickets for Kartya, Bella and myself. We wrote to Kartya's mum announcing our intended arrival. We were so excited to be seeing the whole family in Taiwan, especially Kartya's mum. It had been over four years since Kartya was in Taiwan. She had grown up a lot. She was now a mum herself. The time came for us to leave. Othmar drove us to the airport. It would have been nice if he could come too, but someone had to work.

The flight was uneventful, except for poor little Bella getting an ear ache and screaming half the way there. I looked after her while Kartya slept. We were met at the airport in Taipei by Kartya's sister Jessie and her husband Johnnie. It was a warm emotional reunion. They drove us down to Chinsan to the family home. Everyone was waiting for us. Kartya's mum was so thrilled to see us again. She embraced her daughter and granddaughter warmly. We were all so happy to be together again. Over the next week, we spent every minute with the family. Kartya was reconnecting with brothers, sisters, aunts and other family members. Of course, communication was still a problem. we used a lot of hand language, but no doubt some things were lost in translation.

Kartya's mum wanted to take me to the hairdresser. It was a bit scary when she asked me to hop on the back of her moped. I had never been on a motor bike before. Thank goodness it wasn't too far. When we arrived, everyone in the salon was very interested in meeting Kartya's Australian mama. I thought it was very strange when the young girl started shampooing my hair while I'm sitting up in the chair. My hair wasn't even wet. Oh well, I thought, different country, different way of doing things. After fifteen minutes, she is still shampooing my hair and it's all running down my face and neck. My scalp felt hot from all the rubbing. Eventually she decided to wash it off. I had to stand up with my head bent over the sink while she washed it with the tap. It sure was different. Kartya's mum was getting her hair styled as well. The young girl doing my hair did a lovely job. Very smooth and perfect. When we left the salon to go back home it looked very overcast. Kartya's mum gave me an umbrella in case it rained. Sure enough, half way home it pours down, and it's blowing a gale. I put up the umbrella, trying to shield us both from the rain. That was all good for five minutes, then the umbrella blew inside out. We both started to get very wet. By the time we reached home, we both looked like drowned rats. Bad luck about the beautiful hairstyle. Kartya looked at both her mothers and said, "I thought you went to the hairdresser?" Her mum and I just looked at each other and laughed.

The next day Kartya's mum wanted to take us down to Keelung where Josie, Kartya's cousin lived. It is a major port city situated in the northeastern part of Taiwan. That was all well and good, but she didn't drive. She looked at me? "No, no I couldn't drive, its different side of the road." Kartya piped up, "I'll drive". I said, "No you won't, you can't drive." She was adamant, "Mum its ok, I can drive." Kartya's mum gave her the keys of her big people mover van and we all got in and drove off. I was in the back with Bella and Kartya's two sisters. Kartya's mum was in the front. I was so scared. I had never been in a car with Kartya driving and was not sure if she had any driving skills at all. To make matters worse, it started raining and the windows were fogging up. Kartya's mum was sitting there seemingly unperturbed by the whole thing. She was pointing directions for Kartya. Go this way, go that way. The whole drive down to Keelung was mountains on one side and ocean on the other. The road was wet and slippery and it was still raining. I felt about as anxious as I do when I get on a plane. I had a firm grip on Bella, who was crying and wanting to get in the front with Kartya. Eventually we arrived in Keelung. We drove to Josie's house and picked her up, then we all went shopping. As usual, Kartya was wanting to buy everything she saw. Her mum bought her a white puffy jacket with a fur hood. Kartya looked like an Eskimo in it. After shopping, we all went to eat. I didn't eat much, I couldn't. All I could think of was that we had to drive all the way back and it was still raining. After lunch we all went walking around the city and shops again. I was thinking we should be heading back soon, before it gets dark. No one else seemed concerned, only me. When Josie suggested we all stay for dinner, my heart sank. That would mean we would be driving back in the dark. My thoughts were momentarily diverted, while at dinner I watched little Bella, sitting in her highchair, eating pork ribs marinated in chilli. I thought, yes, like mother like daughter. We eventually headed off home, in the rain and dark. Kartya's mum was sitting beside Kartya, with her eyes closed, sleeping. She was not worried. I have to admit that Kartya was an excellent driver. She delivered us all safe and sound back home. I gave her a hug and congratulated her. I told her I was proud of her. She said, "See mum, I told you there was nothing to worry about".

Kartya's mum is an amazing cook. Kartya definitely got her cooking skills from her mum. Her mum would cook sometimes five different dishes, every one of them delicious. We were very sad when the time came for us to say goodbye. Kartya didn't know when she would see her family again, so there were lots of tears on both sides. It was important for Kartya to experience the love from her family. It was the reassurance she needed, just to know they had not forgotten about her.

When we arrived back in Melbourne, we all went about our own lives. It was not that long after that Othmar was diagnosed with emphysema and Kartya announced she was having another baby. We were not happy about Othmar's diagnosis, but very happy for Kartya and Sam. It would be good for Bella to have a sibling. It was around this time that my brother Brian, invited Othmar to go to Queensland for a holiday. Othmar had never been there in all the time he had lived in Australia. He had a wonderful time hanging out with my brother, but the best thing was his health improved. So much so, that he didn't want to come back home. He could breathe better. He started walking and really enjoyed it. The fresh air and exercise was going to be the key to better health.

When he came back to Melbourne, we discussed the possibility of moving to Queensland. I was keen, but I didn't want to leave Kiersten, Alex, Joshua and Kartya and little Bella. I was worried Bella would forget about us.

When the time came for Kartya to give birth we were all excited about the imminent arrival of another grandchild. Kiersten and myself were in the delivery room, so was Sam. When Kartya gave birth to a little baby boy, we were all elated. They named him Ethan. He was beautiful.

Six months later, Othmar, Joshua and I packed everything up and moved to Queensland. It was one of the best decisions we could have ever made. We loved it from the very beginning. It was the weather that seduced us. When the sun shines most days it is easy to have a smile on your face. We missed the other kids, but it was just a two hour plane flight if we wanted to visit them.

CHAPTER THIRTY-FIVE
Phoenix Rising

Several years later Alex moved to Queensland to be near us. Eventually Kartya, Sam and the two children also moved to Queensland. It was to be a very turbulent few years for us all. Othmar was diagnosed with prostrate cancer. We were so lucky that he was operated on in time and has since recovered.

The relationship between Kartya and Sam broke down irretrievably. Kartya was to become a single mum again. She was faced with the task of bringing up her two children alone.

The first thing she did was go and get a "humongous" tattoo of a phoenix that covered most of her arm and it cost a fortune. This marked her new beginning.

She was also still on methadone. I think it was more the psychological dependence than anything else. She was on such a minute dose that it hardly made a difference. It was more the routine of going to the chemist every day.

It was now time for Kartya to get out in the real world. To be free to discover the person she was meant to be all along; to gain employment in order to support herself and her children. Her skills as a mum were unquestionable. She adored her kids and they adored her. Eventually she gained employment in child care. She was very lucky because it was her first 'real' job at 32 years old. Kartya also discovered spirituality. It changed her life. It was only then that Kartya really started the healing process. She still carried scars and pain from the past. Her feelings of loss and abandonment had abated, but still caused her pain. She would need to do a lot of work on herself to come to a feeling of peace and contentment. I remember when Kartya was about 13, she bought her first tarot deck and a book to teach herself tarot. She always believed there was more of a deeper meaning to life. Especially after all she had been through, she started searching for answers. It was by chance that she met a lady called Sonette from Sonesha Meditation Metaphysics and Vibrational therapies. Kartya was looking for a new house. The area she chose was not really where she wanted to live, but being a single mother you have to take what you can get. It was sheer coincidence that Sonette lived five minutes away. Sonette took Kartya under her wing and encouraged Kartya to become involved in many of her classes. Kartya was like a sponge, absorbing everything about spirituality that she had always believed in.

Kartya once said to me, "Mum, we come here to learn lessons so that we can heal, because if we don't learn to accept and heal from it, we will only hold on to that pain until the day we die."

Kartya learnt to meditate, she has learned Reiki level 1 and 2. Perhaps the lady with the long red hair and the pink kaftan, that had given her Reiki as a teenager had left an impression on her. She also learnt how to connect with her angels, helping her to clear negative and stagnant energy from her being. She is also learning how to heal with crystals. The outcome for Kartya has been to live a very positive life. She no longer has the anger inside that she held onto for so many years. Kartya has found meaning to life with her beloved Isabella and Ethan. She is financially independent, studying, drug free and very healthy. She created a Facebook page called Phoenix Rising with over 18,000 followers. They seek her positive inspirational words on a daily basis. The pain of the past has gone. The happiness of the future will continue.

Epilogue

A word from Kartya …

Whenever I look at my two mothers, the image of their faces inspires me to write about the best eighteenth birthday present that a girl in my position could possibly dream of. Having both my brave mothers inside my mind, my birth mother inspires me to look to my future and my mum inspires me to never give up on what you believe in.

I had always dreamed of finding my birth mother. There were so many questions rolling around in my head. I needed to know the answers to all these questions. Questions that I had been wondering about for so long. Who am I? Where do I come from? Do I have any other family? But the most important: Who is my mother?

Ever since I was twelve I have wanted to know. My Australian mother has always tried to help me, she never stopped trying, always writing letter after letter, no matter what. She never did give up. I guess that's why I love her and appreciate her so much.

It's funny, I remember swearing at her and telling her that she wasn't my real mother. I used to hate her for adopting me. I would say, 'Why didn't you just leave me for dead?' She would say, 'Because we loved you,' but I never believed her.

When I became addicted to heroin, she never gave up on me.

My mum and dad supported me throughout everything. She never thought of disowning me. She never thought to herself, 'Fuck Kartya, she's turned to drugs, we don't need her in our lives.' She just never left my side.

My parents are strong, especially my mother, and she'll never give up on her family or anything she believes in.

When I wasn't living at home, I would ring my mum and abuse her and then just hang up on her. For some reason I had to ring her and abuse her. I felt insecure without her, I needed to always hear her motherly kind of voice. My mum had nonstop loving for me and I must have needed to hear her worry about me. I still have to have contact with her every day. Maybe I have to do it just to check if she is OK each day.

My mother and father tried to get me off heroin, but I would tell them to leave me alone. They could see that I was physically deteriorating, at one stage I got really sick. I lost over ten kilos in two weeks. I weighed fifty-eight kilos and went down to under thirty kilos in about four weeks. I knew that if I didn't make the trip to Taiwan then I would have died. I was in so much pain. No-one could have ever understood, not even my closest friends. I felt like my heart wouldn't stop bleeding and I felt like I didn't want to live. It was a pain that only heroin could take away. That's the only thing that couldn't hurt me. When I first saw my birth mother, all the pain went. It was as if I knew all along what she was like, because it felt like her. When she hugged me, I felt like it was my mother. It felt like someone opened the door of my heart and let all the pain out.

If your child is adopted like me, and has problems, they may want to find their family. Don't be scared in helping because, no matter what happens, your adopted child will still love you the most, because you are the one that brought them up. You would never lose your child to their birth parents.

A word from Nola …

Kartya's journey has been long and at times arduous for herself and the whole family. We are proud of Kartya for overcoming many obstacles in her life that only a very strong person could conquer.

> *Thank you for voicing your pain at a very early age and forcing us to act upon it. Too many adoptees hide their pain and carry it inside for years. You were the catalyst to us not only finding your family, but also Kiersten's. If it was not for you, we may not have tried, thinking it to be impossible. You forced us to come out of the fog and acknowledge the pain and heartache that can be caused through adoption. You have been like a caterpillar emerging from the chrysalis and becoming a beautiful butterfly.*

We are proud of Kiersten, Alex and Joshua who have stood by and supported Kartya every step of the way. This is what a family should do. Kartya has proven to be an amazing mother to our only two grandchildren Isabella 11 and Ethan 8. They are exceptional, well mannered children and are a credit to her. They are happy well adjusted kids. They are a pleasure to have around. Kartya's story is proof that no matter how difficult one's journey becomes, with hard work and commitment, with love and support from family, nothing is impossible. Kartya has a peace and serenity about her today that we have never seen before. May her journey of recovery continue.

Kartya and sister Ja-chi in front of the media.
The pain and sadness is evident.

Kartya's third meeting with her birth mother, Li-meng and sister, Ja-chi.
Kartya is overjoyed.

*Nola and Othmar with Kartya and their beloved
grandchildren, Bella and Ethan*

About the Author

Nola Wunderle was born and raised in Geelong, Victoria, Australia. One of ten children, she was a young girl when she made the decision to adopt a child one day. It was a passionate desire of hers. Little did she realise that later she would be just as passionate about finding her adopted daughter's birth mother.

Nola has an abiding interest in international adoption and supports a number of organisations and initiatives that work for the empowerment of women:

- *ACT* Against Child Trafficking
- *Destiny Rescue*, who rescue children out of the sex trade
- *Somaly Mam Foundation* who empower survivors of forced sexual slavery
- *Petals in the Dust*, a documentary film project that aims to help girls and woman who are victims of discrimination, violence and "gendercide" in India.

She lives on the Gold Coast in Queensland with her husband.

We support Against Child Trafficking (ACT) it is a non profit organisation registered in the Netherlands.

ACT works to prevent child trafficking for intercountry adoption and assists victims in getting justice.

Visit their website and give them your support.
http://www.againstchildtrafficking.org

CPSIA information can be obtained
at www.ICGtesting.com
Printed in the USA
BVHW08s1715080818
523917BV00005B/158/P

9 780992 273408